Collecting
TIN TOYS

Collecting
TIN TOYS

JACK TEMPEST

New Cavendish Books
London

Pincushion Press
Tampa

DEDICATION

To Martin, Julie and Andrew

and to all those who have helped me enjoy the facinating hobby of toy collecting by providing information, finding me interesting items and allowing me to visit their personal collections including:

François Alary, Dr Colin Baddiel, Klaus Banke, Ira Bernstein, Bob Blake, Franco Boscia, Irving Brim, Jacky Broutin, Mike Butler, Pierce Carlson, Count Giansanti Coluzzi, Andrés Diego, Peter Dunk, Jock Farquharson, Dave Finn, Mike Foster, Peter Geissler, Robert Gerard, Jacky Gondry, David Gordon, Jack Herbert, Giles Hervé, Peter A. Jäger, François Jammet, Hilary Kay, Dale Kelley, Philippe de Lespinay, Kevin McGimpsey and Stewart Orr of the Chester Toy Museum, the late Peter Ottenheimer, David Pressland, Geoff Price, Jacques Remise, Dr Bill Souter, Kurt Strebel, Kenneth Sutcliffe and the late R. J. A. Thomson.

Also, to all the Peter Pans of this world who appreciate the charm and ingenuity of bygone playthings-especially if they are made from tinplate!

British Library Cataloguing in Publication Data

Tempest, Jack
    Collecting tin toys. – (Collecting series).
    1. Tin toys – Collectors and collecting
    I. Title
    688.7'2   TS2301.T7

Printed and bound in Hong Kong under the supervision of Mandarin Offset.

New Cavendish Books Ltd.
3 Denbigh Road
London W11 2SJ

ISBN 1 872727 66 2 (UK edition)

Published in the USA by
Pincushion Press
5245 Baywater Drive
Tampa, FL 33615

ISBN 1 883685 02 8 (US edition)

Design: Peter Wrigley

FRONTISPIECE

Maker	Unknown (possibly Hoch & Beckmann)
Marks	Unmarked
Date	c. 1900
Height	8 ³/₄ in (22cm)

Although no maker's name appears on this clockwork toy roundabout with airplanes and airships, similar items appear in the German Moko catalogues from the early years of the century. The clockwork is tensioned by sliding the lever in the base the roundabout should have a flag on top, but sadly this was mislaid during the photographic session. These items are generally difficult to find. This example is rather plain; the more colourful and decorative the artwork, the more desirable these pieces are.

Courtesy Chester Toy and Doll Museum

CONTENTS

FOREWORD

Rather like Philip Larkin's description of another pleasurable activity a decade or so earlier, collecting Tin Toys began in 1976!

That year saw the publication of David Pressland's seminal work, The Art of the Tin Toy which had a profound effect on raising awareness of the richness and diversity of tin toys stretching back from the 1970s to the nineteenth century.

Of course toys made of tin, decorated with enamel or lithography had been collected pre-Pressland. However their 'tinniness', particularly in the collection of toy trains had been an ancilliary factor, notwithstanding the wide use of the word 'tinplate' which commonly described their course scale as distinct from the tin, diecast and steel from which they were made.

Prior to the mid-seventies tin toy collection with the exception of trains was almost exclusively concerned with German-made items. The inclusion of a chapter on post-Second World War toys in David's book changed all that. As David's editor at that time I was instrumental in the inclusion of that chapter and indeed the passion with which David subsequently built up a Japanese tin toy car collection was awesome. As often in life the preacher did not heed his own words, but that's another story.

As obsolescence and collectability become ever more condensed the tin toy treasures of the 1950s and 1970s have in many instances acheived parity in both value and rarity with their illustrious forebears. Collecting Tin Toys pulls the strands of this topic together with great clarity and knowledge.

Jack Tempest, a well-known figure in the world of toy collecting over many years, has written a concise and thoughtfully researched book which is a worthy addition to the publisher's excellent paperback 'Collecting Series'.

Allen Levy
Co-Founder and former
Director of The London Toy
and Model Museum
London 1994

INTRODUCTION

Collecting toys is an immensely popular hobby nowadays, and one that keeps innumerable specialized toy fairs – "swap meets" as they are generally known – regularly attracting busy crowds week in and week out and feeding the enthusiasms of toy collectors throughout the world.

But *why* are the toys of bygone days so desirable to own? There is, of course, in all of us an inexplicable "magpie" streak that the hobby helps to satisfy, whether it is manifested in collections of toy trains or cars or character figures. There is also the aesthetic aspect of collecting examples of past craftsmanship, for the toys of yesteryear generally display far greater qualities of workmanship, decoration and ingenuity in their mechanical actions than do their modern counterparts. They also act as tiny three-dimensional time capsules, bringing with them across the years much of the craftsmanship of a long-vanished way of life, together with some of its atmosphere. Turn-of-the century toys, for instance, are particularly evocative of the period in which they were made. Steam railways and stations, ocean liners, "horseless-carriages" and the flying machines that were to follow, were all produced in wonderfully detailed, scaled-down form, many examples having survived to act as miniaturized reminders of a pioneering age of invention.

However, perhaps the main reason people collect tin toys is the joy of pure nostalgia, as memories of our forever lost childhood are rekindled

Left-hand toy
Maker **Unknown American**
Marks **None**
Date **1940s**
Length **10in (26cm)**
"Let the Drummer Boy play while you swing and sway," says the message on the drum. The Drummer Boy beats the drum as the clockwork-powered toy trundles along. This is another of those toys that is soon given a home in any collection of novelty toys but that is difficult to find.

Right-hand toy
Maker **Marx**
Marks *Marx*
Date **1940s**
Length **9in (23cm)**
Also typically American is the "Charlie McCarthy" car, a version of the pirouetting "whoopee car". A character toy, this has a wider appeal to American collectors who hold nostalgic memories of Charlie McCarthy, Edgar Bergen's ventriloquial dummy. Quite rare. *Sotheby's*

Clockwork musical clowns by Günthermann of Nuremburg.

A clockwork diver by Bing: the toy, which stands 8½in (21.5cm) high, dives automatically in the water and rises again to the surface.

when we have an opportunity to handle once again a well-remembered favourite toy. It is such memories, perhaps recalled by a chance sighting of a once-owned toy in an antique shop window or on a swap meet stall, that have so often been responsible for triggering off a desire to embark upon the intriguing pastime of toy collecting.

Children are not usually credited with being the most careful members of the human race, and it is amazing that so many toys have survived for so many years. It is a tribute not only to the toy makers who produced these comparatively delicate objects but also to the children and parents who owned them that sufficient examples have survived to provide the basis for such a popular and far-flung hobby.

It is only in the years since World War II that toy collecting has become a recognized and respectable activity, but the hobby has grown rapidly as people have begun to realize the monetary values of juvenilia. The leading auction houses, observing the steadily rising demand for old toys by collectors in the late 1960s, arranged specialist sales devoted to items of juvenilia. The resulting media publicity accorded to the high prices being offered for certain items helped to accelerate the growth in interest in toys. Older collectors tend to bemoan this development. They were able to buy cheaply, of course. But they too, no doubt, will be happy enough to use the auctioneers when they come to sell!

From the point of view of investment, toys do appear to offer excellent prospects for the future. As interest in them increases, they are becoming more difficult to find on the market, especially the very early, classical examples, some of which are now almost priceless. No one, of course, can foretell future developments and demands, but the outlook does look promising. Many people are diverting funds to the purchase of rare toys, and a number of them readily raise bids in the thousands of pounds at auctions. Rare toys in first-class condition are the best investment, of course, but restored pieces (expertly finished) are reasonably desirable, provided that a good proportion of the original toy remains. If the toy in question is a particularly rare example, so much the better. Today, specialized auctions attract dealers and collectors from many countries. Nevertheless, although prices achieved in the saleroom may be high, it is still possible to find bargains here and there, even at auctions, and all collectors dream of finding an attic full of forgotten Victorian playthings – which can, and does, happen occasionally.

Some people wonder why one toy is more collectable than another. Obviously, the majority of rare playthings are desirable, but if they fall within a particular collecting area they may be even more desirable than other, equally scarce items. The fever to possess certain toys is generally focused in a number of clearly defined directions. For example, there is widespread interest in the products of many of the early German toy manufacturers. Equally well-made toys, from, say, Italian toy makers, have tended to lag behind in the collecting stakes, although their quality often equals that of their German equivalents and they can be even harder to find because they were produced in far smaller quantities, being

kept mainly for home consumption. Once hardly acknowledged by collectors outside Italy, they are now especially desirable.

Present-day safety regulations discourage the sale of toys made from tinplate because many of the cheaper products tend to have dangerously sharp edges. These restrictions may be a factor in the growth of collecting this type of toy, human nature generally desiring that which is forbidden. But if you are starting from scratch and want to speculate in currently produced toys, you will have to settle for plastic and diecast items. Diecast toys are subject to regulations forbidding the use of lead both in their construction and in the paint with which they are decorated, but alternative alloys are available.

The diecast collector is fortunate in being able to collect from manufacturers' current output, and he is thus able to begin a collection quite inexpensively from a very wide range of predominantly automotive items. Nostalgia is satisfied by the issue of a variety of classic vintage and veteran car models, some produced as "limited editions", which suggests that they may, one day, become valuable. Only time will tell.

With no modern tinplate toys available, apart from the occasional crude and uninteresting examples that seem to find their way from the Far East, collectors must remain content with the products of the past. They need not necessarily go back to Victorian times to find them as

Maker **Stock**
Marks **Crossed walking sticks in a circle**
Date **1920s–1930s**
Length **7¾in (20cm)**
This is a well-known German toy, made by the firm of Stock, which tended to style some of its clockwork tinplate novelties after Lehmann's products. As the toy travels along, the driver waves his stick, slackening and tightening the reins alternately. These toys occasionally appear on the market, often in mint condition and with the original boxes.

many interesting metal toys were produced between 1950 and 1970. For example, the old established Spanish firm Paya, which is still in business, is currently busily producing attractive reproductions of many of its early models. These have to be clearly labelled as "collectors' models" to meet the import and sales requirements of many countries. They may not be sold to children, although their prices would, in any case, be prohibitive. These, like many diecast models, are being produced in "limited editions", and they may have a certain investment value, although there are no guarantees.

Japan was the last of the great toy-making countries, its massive output in the immediate post-World War II years eclipsing Germany's previous domination of world markets. Japanese manufacturers turned out a wonderful variety of metal toys during the 1950s and 1960s, and all were made to a high standard of workmanship. In the 1930s, on the other hand, Japanese toys were generally inferior and tended to include quantities of celluloid combined with the tinplate. Celluloid is highly flammable and is not allowed in toy or doll making today.

A toy is an item intended for children, primarily for their amusement but also for their education. It can teach many things during the formative years and also help to develop the sense of pride of possession. Toys can lead a child from the world of imagination into the realms of reality. Today, the values of "educational" toys are stressed, just as the Victorians once introduced their offspring to the miracles of the Steam Age by providing them with "scientific" toys such as simple live-steam engines, both locomotive and stationary. The point at which a child's toy becomes a collector's item is difficult to define. Some toys have been discovered after being stored away for many years. Others have grown desirable comparatively quickly; the tinplate products of Japan are an example: in the shops in the 1950s to 1970s, some of these, especially examples of the space toys and robots, already command quite high prices.

While the individual collector may have his or her own personal reasons for pursuing the hobby, the thrill of discovering a rare item is shared by all. It is the hard-to-find piece that adds spice to the whole interest. American toy collector Al Marwick summed it up: "the fun is in the search!"

Maker **Bandai**
Marks **Gothic B in a C**
Date **1960s**
Length **13in (33cm)**
A "Kingsize" Cadillac by the Japanese firm Bandai. This opulent car is equipped with light-up headlamps, working steering-wheel, horn, three forward gears and reverse gear. An ideal toy for any boy! Toys like this, although not "antiques" in any sense of the word, are becoming more difficult to buy, largely because of the activities of automotive collectors.

1.
COLLECTING

Toy collecting is basically the same the world over, varying only in nostalgic appeal for locally produced, indigenous items. Our sentimental memories of childhood differ not only, of course, from person to person but also from country to country as the toys locally available varied. German-made toys were known to more children than the products of other countries because they were exported in such large quantities all over the world. The toys of other nations, often patriotically encouraged as part of a general effort to combat the ever-increasing importation of goods of all kinds from Germany, tended to be popular mainly within their country of origin and were exported in only limited quantities.

Although some American products were sent to Britain, they never attained the popularity of German imports. A British child who received, say, a Lionel train set as a present, would have been in the minority. More likely, he would have been given one of the popular Hornby train sets or perhaps an example originating from a German manufacturer. The memory of this childhood possession would tend to stay with him for life,

Left-hand toy
Maker **Unknown**
Marks *Stollwerk Bros. Cologne. Germany*
Date **Early 1900s**
Height **6¼in (16cm)**

Right-hand toy
Maker **Unknown**
Marks *Made in Germany*
Date **Early 1900s**
Height **4¾in (12cm)**

The left-hand example of these two tinplate money-boxes (or banks) earned the coin placed in the slot by issuing a tiny bar of Stollwerk Chocolate. The toy was made specifically for the Stollwerk Chocolate Co. to promote its chocolate. It is hard to find. The right-hand money-box, the figure of a ragged tramp, just sits and begs for your money. The slot is in his chest, above a notice that reads:

Poor Weary Willie
I'm a comical knave
But your money I'll save.
The more you give ME
The richer YOU'LL be.

A difficult-to-find item. Both examples are nicely lithographed.

and it is natural that British collectors prefer to collect the products of the Hornby factory (or German trains) rather than the lesser known, but equally excellent, offerings, that issued from Lionel.

Such nostalgia can be passed on from father to son, even when the goods have long since disappeared from the shops. Hornby products are particularly collectable in Britain, and an active Hornby Collectors' Club, which has members from all over the world, exists to support the interest. The main interest is in gauge O, but the Dublo range has become increasingly collectable over the last few years.

Toy collecting really began to be popular in the 1960s and 1970s, and toy fairs were organized primarily in response to a widespread interest in automotive diecast models. A few tinplate toys may have appeared on some of the stalls, but the main business was the buying, selling and exchanging of diecast toys. The name "swap meet" became a popular description of these events, which have grown rapidly as ever-increasing numbers of people have taken up the hobby. Toy fairs are now a regular feature of the way of life of collectors in Britain, the rest of Europe and North America, and frequent events are staged. Many collectors and dealers travel all over the world to attend these specialized shows, which now generally include a much higher percentage of tinplate toys than in the early days.

Toy collecting is a complex subject, and the beginner may well be advised to consider theme collecting so that there is some uniformity among the items accumulated. Toy railways are a typical example, and perhaps a few examples of Dinky Toys, diecast farm animals and other miniatures could be added for visual effect.

Specializing in toy trains usually means sticking to one particular gauge, although the output of different manufacturers may occupy the lay-out. Electric trains are less trouble to control over a large area of track, but some people prefer to concentrate on clockwork-powered locomotives. Realistically designed lay-outs, complete with stations, buildings and scenery are perhaps the ideal solution to the problems of displaying model railways, but this takes up quite a bit of space, especially if gauge O items are collected.

It is perhaps important to note at this point the difference between "toys" and "models". The two words are often used as synonyms. Strictly speaking, however, they are quite different. A toy is manufactured purely as a plaything and usually in large quantities; a model is normally painstakingly created as a carefully scaled-down image of its original, whether it is produced commercially or privately by an enthusiast making no real difference. Commercial models are generally made singly or in limited quantities, often for demonstration or publicity purposes. Toy collectors are, in the main, not too interested in items that have not been produced by toy manufacturers. The opposite applies to model enthusiasts, who are more concerned with exactness of detail and scale.

Exactness of scale and detail are not important to children who tend to live in a world of dreams and make-believe, but toy makers have turned

Maker **Nomura Toys**
Marks **None on toy; *TN* [in a diamond] on the box**
Date **1950s–1960s**
Height **7½in (19cm)**
This figure is popularly known as "Eat at Joe's" although its real name is "Ko-Ko, the Mechanical Sandwich Man". The English version carries a sandwich-board reading "Eat at Joe's. Steak. Hamburger. Delicious", but here is the Italian version, which is rarer, at least in the U.K. Made in Japan of tinplate with fabric clothing and a vinyl head, "Eat at Joe's" will wobble about, twitch his nose and raise his hat when the mechanism is wound up. A popular collectors' toy and one that is difficult to find today.

Maker **Unknown German**
Marks *Made in Germany*
Date *c.1908*
Length 15in (38cm)

This fascinating carpet toy is known as the "Champion Scullers", and the oarsmen "row" realistically as the toy travels across the floor. A rare toy and one that has enormous appeal for all collectors. *Sotheby's*

OPPOSITE
Maker **Märklin**
Marks *G.M. & Cie.* [intertwined] in a shield
Date 1902–9
Dimensions 15¼×20¾×11¾in (39×53×30cm)

This beautiful toy railway station is just one of the various styles that Gebrüder Märklin made. Some were even larger, but all displayed the first-class manufacturing qualities of this leading firm of toy makers. The detail is clearly to be seen on the photograph – even to the telegraph insulators, which marked the invention of this new form of signalling. The language of the notices was changed to suit the countries to which Märklin exported. This station is rare.

out some realistic items, especially railway locomotives and rolling stock, which may be almost worthy of being classed as models. These more lifelike items were intended for older children, who were developing an appreciation of the real thing, and probably for their parents, too, who supplied the money!

Toy- or model-railway lay-outs can take up a great deal of room, but there are many smaller toys on which to focus. Finding examples of these should not be too expensive, especially the ones that originated from Japan in the 1950s and onwards. They can be models of vehicles and motor-cycles or simply colourful novelties of all kinds – somersaulting figures, crazy cars, pecking birds and so on. The themes can be narrowed even further: a collection might be solely composed of toys featuring, say, monkeys or circus clowns.

Another idea would be to concentrate on collecting the products of a particular manufacturer. One firm that particularly appeals to many collectors is Schuco, a Nuremberg company that produced a fascinating range of novelty animated toys over the years. Another German firm that issued many novelty toys is Lehmann; these are not cheap toys, but it would be still possible to build up an accumulation of quite a range of examples. Collecting Märklin products would be difficult – and expensive. The firm's toys are particularly sought after by Germans, and they are rarely – if ever – seen on toy fair stalls nowadays as they usually end up in the auction houses.

The British firm of Tri-ang introduced a range of neat little clockwork-powered tinplate road vehicles in the 1930s, which would make an ideal subject for collecting. They are not too hard to find at toy fairs and often come up in auction. Some items in the range are, of course, more difficult to find than others, but that simply adds interest to the hobby.

Always worth looking out for are the trade catalogues and other ephemera related to tinplate toys (or any toys for that matter). These catalogues, which are usually well-illustrated, can be invaluable sources of information on the subject of bygone toys. They were often published by the manufacturers themselves and sometimes also by trade ware-houses or department stores. The two latter types do not always publicize the actual manufacturers of the items but they invariably illustrate and usefully date the various toys.

Maker **Mettoy**
Marks *Made in England* printed on the box
Date **c.1950**
Length **7in (18cm)**
This North American Indian is riding a
motorcycle in full regalia, including a
feathered head-dress. The brightly coloured
clockwork toy, which is of tin (except for the
Indian's plastic head), is called "Big Chief".
Difficult to find.

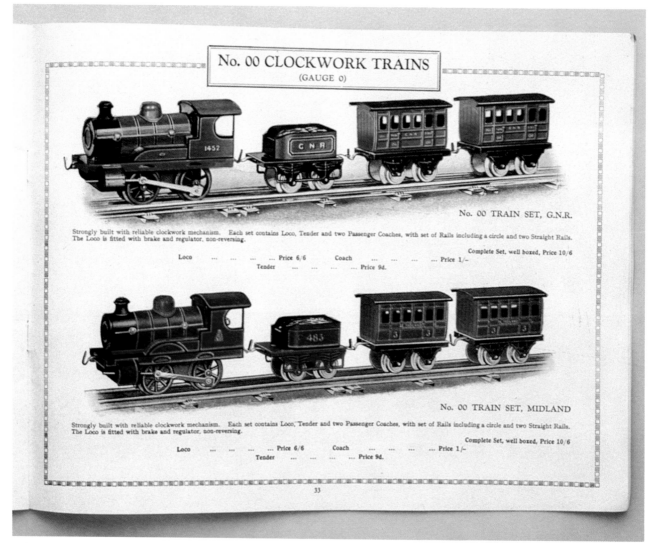

No. 00 CLOCKWORK TRAINS
(GAUGE 0)

No. 00 TRAIN SET, G.N.R.

Strongly built with reliable clockwork mechanism. Each set contains Loco, Tender and two Passenger Coaches, with set of Rails including a circle and two Straight Rails. The Loco is fitted with brake and regulator, non-reversing.

Complete Set, well boxed, Price 10/6

Loco ... ... Price 6/6   Coach ... ... Price 1/-
Tender ... ... Price 9d.

No. 00 TRAIN SET, MIDLAND

Strongly built with reliable clockwork mechanism. Each set contains Loco, Tender and two Passenger Coaches, with set of Rails including a circle and two Straight Rails. The Loco is fitted with brake and regulator, non-reversing.

Complete Set, well boxed, Price 10/6

Loco ... ... Price 6/6   Coach ... ... Price 1/-
Tender ... ... Price 9d.

33

ABOVE
This colourful early catalogue advertising the famous British-made Hornby Trains appeared shortly after the end of World War I. The page illustrated shows some of the lower-priced range, which bear a remarkable resemblance to some of the models made by the German firm Bing. Although no proof has been discovered of any connection between Gebrüder Bing and Hornby, the similarities are striking.

RIGHT
Collecting catalogues can be almost as interesting as collecting the toys themselves, and all catalogues are worth picking up, if the opportunity arises, even if only to pass on to someone interested in research.
    The catalogue illustrated here, which was published by Lines Brothers in the 1930s, shows a wide range of the firm's products – including part of its wonderful range of miniature tinplate clockwork road vehicles produced in its Minic series.

2815

S. SERIES O and OO
OO and OOO, but on' elevat...
to occupy minimum space. S...
× 5¾" × 5". Height of OO 9½"...

L.B.L.
DOCK CRANE

2820

DOCK CRANE
, on four steel wheels. Working...
with chain winding gear. Crane...
. Very strong and well finished...
given with jib folded.

MINIC ALL TO SCALE CLOCKWORK TOYS

Almost every type of vehicle on the road represented; some with electric lights. Strongly constructed, and fitted with powerful, long-running mechanism, they will run anywhere, **even on the carpet.** Disc wheels, with rubber tyres. Each model is beautifully finished in a variety of colours, and packed singly in an attractive box. Various quantities according to type are packed in strong outer fibre cases for transit.

2845 MINIC Light Tank. Length 3½".

2922 MINIC Ford Royal Mail Van. Length 3½".

2821 MINIC Ford £100 Saloon. Length 3½".

2823 MINIC Ford Light Van. Length 3½".

2835 MINIC Tractor. Length 3".

2842 Vauxhall Cabriolet.

2841 Vauxhall Town Coupé.

2840 Vauxhall Tourer.

2851. Tourer with Passengers.

2824 MINIC Sports Saloon. Length 4¼".

2856 MINIC Mechanical Horse and Trailer with cases. Length 7½".

2830 MINIC Streamline Sports. Length 5".

2825 MINIC Limousine. Length 4¼".

2826 MINIC Cabriolet. Length 4¼".

2866 MINIC Double-deck 'Bus. Length 7½". Red or Green.

2827 MINIC Town Coupé. Length 4¼".

2831 MINIC Learner's Car. Length 4¼".

2834 MINIC Delivery Lorry. Length 5½".

2862 MINIC Single-deck 'Bus. Length 7½". Red or Green.

2839 MINIC Tip Lorry. Length 5½".

2861 MINIC Searchlight Lorry with electric searchlight and battery. Length 5½"

2865 MINIC Caravan Set (Tourer with passengers and Caravan with electric light). Overall length 9½".
2857 MINIC Caravan with electric light and battery. Length 4¼".

2860 MINIC Breakdown Lorry with Mechanical Crane. Length 5½".

2.
A BRIEF HISTORY OF
TIN TOYS

The coming of the Industrial Revolution in the 19th century led to a gradual all-round increase in the availability of a wide variety of products and a subsequent steady rise in the general standard of living. It was at this period of history that tinplate toys began to appear on the market.

Before this time, toys for the poorer classes were much simpler; they were usually naïve, home-made wooden products such as crude dolls for the girls and bats and balls for the boys. Among the wealthy, curiously enough, many of the toys were intended for the amusement of the head of the family. Such toys were produced with great ingenuity by specialist automata makers during the 18th and early 19th centuries, and some, decorated with precious metals and gems, were designed to be the playthings of kings and princes.

Originally, the word "toy" was used to describe trifling novelties or small objects. Early needlework tools, for instance, were known as toys. The verb "to toy" still echoes this meaning, and the expression "toying around" has nothing to do with playing. In his book *Children's Toys Throughout the Ages*, Leslie Daiken suggests that the word's origins lie in the Old English verb *teon*, meaning to draw or to lead, which may have been applied to the pull-along type of toy. Perhaps a more likely explanation of its derivation lies in the Scandinavian influence on the English language, the Danish equivalent of "plaything" being *legetøj*. *Lege*, meaning "to play", is still a commonly used dialect word in the north-east of England, pronounced as "laik"; *to laik football* is a common example.

With the advent of mass production and the appearance on the market of playthings, it would be natural for wholesalers to list such items in their trade catalogues under the heading "toys", along with all the other small novelties, accessories and gewgaws.

A trade catalogue for 1826 illustrates toys made from various materials, including tinplate, and in 1851, at the Great Exhibition in London, tinplate toys were exhibited for the first time. These early toys were hand made and created originally from wooden prototypes, from which skilled tinsmiths formed the metal parts of the toys. Machine presses duplicated the resulting different components. The lacquering and hand painting of details was completed by women, before the parts were assembled, clockwork mechanisms added and the toys hand soldered ready for despatch.

Much of the world's toy trade was based in the Nuremberg area of

LEFT
Toy manufacturers seemed to enjoy producing the occasional weird insect. This group of German toys illustrates some of the more bizarre. In the foreground is an ingenious wing-flapping, walking beetle made by Lehmann in the early years of this century. The large ladybird, by Günthermann, is 7in (18cm) long. The other two carry no trademark, and the smallest one, a simple penny toy, is only 2¾in (7cm) long. These items occasionally crop up at auction sales.

Betriebsmodelle zu Dampfmaschinen und Motoren

in bester mechanischer Ausführung und feinster Lackierung.

No. 697
Bergbahn

No. 924
Bergbahn

No. 970
Farbenrad

No. 912
Trommler

No. 699
Baumsäge

No. 974
Leuchtrad.

No. 915
Mann am Biertisch

No. 685
Kaserne

No. 686
Unterstand

Bavaria, where skilled workers, accustomed to engineering in miniature for such trades as watch and thimble making and for the manufacture of musical instruments, were readily available. Among the factories established in Nuremberg were Bing (founded in 1863–5), Carette (1886), Issmayer (1861), Plank (1866) and Schoenner (1875).

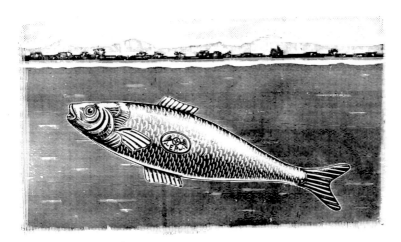

In France at the same period similar methods were used, but hand soldering was retained long after other countries had adopted the more convenient method of using clips or tabs and slots to connect the metal sections. The method of toy production in the United States was similar, but the toys were generally finished in a more colourful style, although the actual make up of the products tended to have a less detailed finish than those of their European counterparts.

In the early days of toy production European manufacturers recruited workers to carry out part-time work in their own homes. Hard work was rewarded with low wages, the workers usually having to provide their own raw materials scavenged from any pieces of scrap metal they could unearth – rubbish dumps were a favourite place to search for discarded food cans, which had to be cleaned before they could be recycled into toys. Prisoners in the local gaols were often used as cheap labour.

An important advance in mass-production methods was the development towards the end of the 18th century of a suitable technique for printing onto metal sheets. When exactly the machinery was brought into use by the Nuremberg toy makers is not definitely known, but its introduction was a great impetus to production, and the skilled hand painters eventually became redundant.

Printing directly onto metal sheets is, as may be appreciated, a more difficult task than printing onto pliable paper, a material more sympathetic to mechanical handling. Moreover, paper possesses the useful property of being able to absorb the ink used while metal does not. The invention of lithography in Bavaria, by Alois Senefelder in 1798 went a long way towards solving the problem. The idea depended on the simple

OPPOSITE
A selection of toys from the German company, Doll & Cie., illustrated in a 1920s catalogue. All these toys were designed to be operated by hand or from a belt-drive conducting power from a steam engine.

LEFT
Here's a novelty: a clockwork fish that actually swims! Made by Plank, whose trademark is clearly visible on the side of the fish, in the 1920s, it is 8¾in (22cm) long.

Maker **Carette**
Marks *G.C.N.Co.*
Date 1900–14
Length 12½in (32cm)

Georges Carette was a Frenchman who started to manufacture toys in Nuremberg in 1886. This landaulette is a fine example of the company's earlier products. It is well detailed, with opening doors, a folding leather hood over the rear seats, and a glazed windscreen. It is very rare.

fact that water and oil are incompatible. The original design is executed on the flat surface of a porous lithographic limestone slab and then the whole dampened with water. The lithographic stone would accept ink only where the design, executed in oil-paint, had repelled the water. The remaining dampened areas, in turn, refused to accept the oil-based ink.

Original applications of this process were used to provide the basic outline of the design, any colour being added by hand afterwards. Printing in colour came later when Godefroye Engelmann patented a system of chromolithography in Paris in 1837. The quality of the finished design depended on the number of colours used to build up the final illustration. Up to a dozen or so colours could be used, and as each colour required its own stone, each area of a particular colour had to be drawn accurately on a separate stone. Printing these stones accurately in sequence built up the final design. Some beautiful results could be obtained by using several colours. Colour shading effects and densities were obtained by the artist's painting an area in dots. Other colours were obtainable by this method – blue dots printed over a yellow surface gave a green effect, for example.

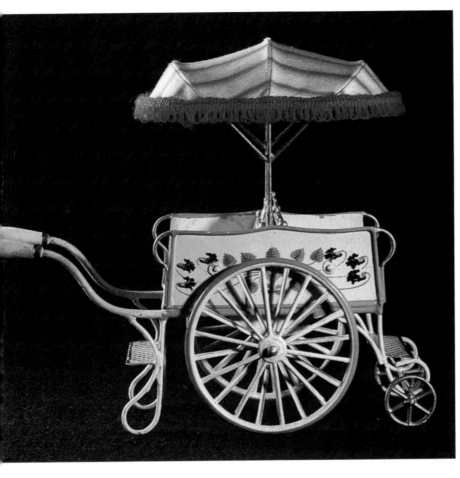

Maker   **Märklin**
Marks   *G.M. & Cie.* [intertwined] in a
            shield
Date   *c.*1909
Dimensions 10½×3¾×8in
          (27×9.5×21cm)

This beautifully ornamented baby carriage is designed to allow its young owner to transport two of her smaller dolls. The seats are movable so that the passengers can travel facing one another or back to back. Made in the usual Märklin way, this perambulator is a marvellous piece of workmanship and is very rare.

Printing direct onto unyielding tinplate still presented its problems, but the solution came in the 1860s when designs were printed directly onto paper and then transferred to the metal. This was achieved by fixing the printed paper to the metal under pressure and then soaking away the paper to leave the decoration securely attached to the surface. The transfers used today by model-makers to add realistic decoration to their miniature trains and road vehicles and by children to ornament their scrapbooks (and bare arms) work in exactly the same way.

This was the earliest form of offset printing, a technique that was eventually improved during the second half of the 19th century by the introduction of a glazed cardboard or rubber cylinder to effect the transfer of the design directly onto the metal. This resulted in a great speeding up of production.

The results of all these processes of decoration can be seen on the toys of different periods. The quality of the chromolithographic decoration is especially beautiful, particularly when a number of colours have been used during printing. Even some of the cheaply produced penny toys

Four penny toys – so called after their original price. There are many varieties of these tiny tin toys, which measured between 3 and 4in (8–10cm) in length. They were produced by a number of German toy makers, and the majority of them were beautifully made and lithographed. Some had simple movements – wheeled vehicles may be assisted by a fly-wheel drive, and the gnomes (on the left) hammer the anvil by operating a "to and fro" sliding mechanism. These toys were made around the turn of the century. *Courtesy Chester Toy and Doll Museum*

LEFT
A close-up of the rocking-horse penny toy showing the detailed lithography that was used to adorn even these cheap toys.
Courtesy Chester Toy and Doll Museum

RIGHT
Maker **Märklin**
Marks ***G.M. & Cie.* [intertwined] in a shield**
Date *c.*1909
Length 17¾in (45cm)
All the charm of the turn-of-the-century fairground is captured in this wonderfully evocative carousel. The detail in the design and presentation is exquisite, and altogether it is a toy of great charm and beauty. It can be revolved by winding the wheel at the side by hand or by a transmission belt from a model steam engine. Delightful and very rare.

display excellent examples of chromolithographic printing, which offers both an appealing depth of colour and detailed design.

Making figures that move mysteriously has obsessed man for centuries. Early philosophers produced images of men, birds and insects that were given movement by hydraulic pressure or heat or by the simple expedients of placing mercury or small beetles into sealed passages within the figure. The flow of the heavy liquid metal or the movement of the insect attempting to escape gave the figures apparent movement.

The "scientific toys" of the Steam Age of the 19th century were regarded as educational necessities for the young boys of the period. Simple steam engines appeared on the market, stationary as well as in trains and boats. Gradually improvements were made towards the turn of the century when steam engines even appeared built into toy motor cars. German manufacturers produced a great variety of stationary steam engines, which could be used to drive, by means of belt and pulleys, fairground carousels or even to operate picturesque working-model water fountains!

Some of the cheap tin penny toy type boats that appeared on the market from Germany and Japan in the 1930s were operated by a very simple water-circulation motor consisting of little more than a U-shaped metal tube heated by a piece of birthday-cake candle. They were known as "pop-pop" or "toc-toc" boats because of the sound they made as they chugged along the water. The British firm of Sutcliffe used a similar, although better designed, form of the same engine to power its original toy boats, which were offered for sale in the 1920s.

The inertia motor is little more than a heavy flywheel, which can be made to spin rapidly by friction. The rapidly spinning wheel, linked to a toy car's road wheels, will carry it forward quite a distance before it slows down. It is a cheaper form of mechanism than a clockwork motor and is

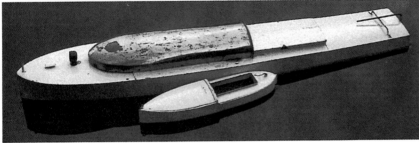

Left-hand toy

Maker	**Unknown German**
Marks	**None**
Date	**Early 1900s**
Height	**14in (36cm)**

The carousel is a typical example of a turn-of-the-century toy from Germany. Such toys were usually powered by clockwork and were often fitted with a musical movement. The colourful decoration adds interest and value to these rarer toys.

Right-hand toy

Maker	**Müller & Kadeder**
Marks	**M.K. [and hot air balloon]**
Date	**c.1905**
Height	**13in (33cm)**

The Ferris wheel or "Russian carousel" is hand painted and has five gondolas. It was designed to be powered from a stationary steam engine. Like most of these early products this is a desirable – and rare – toy.

Sotheby's

Front ship

Maker	**Sutcliffe**
Marks	*Sutcliffe*
Date	**1920s**
Length	**6in (15cm)**

Rear ship

Maker	**Sutcliffe**
Marks	*Sutcliffe*
Date	**1930s**
Length	**3ft 3in (1m)**

Pictured here are the largest and the smallest of the boats produced by Sutcliffe Pressings of Leeds. The smaller of the two was among the earliest to be manufactured, and it was powered by the water-circulating "toc-toc" system. The larger boat is a rare survivor of a battery-powered craft produced in the 1930s for a limited period. Since the closure of the Sutcliffe factory in the early 1980s, collectors have shown more interest in its products. The earlier models are quite rare, although the later examples, produced right up to the factory's closure, are relatively easy to find.

Mike Butler collection

suitable for certain toys. Earlier motors of this kind were often fitted with a pulley around which strong thread was wound. A quick pull set the wheel spinning merrily – gyroscopic tops, which operate by the same method, are still available today.

Occasionally a toy has appeared that uses an elastic-band as a source of power. This simple power source was best suited to powering lightweight model aircraft, if only because of its simplicity and lightness. Gravity has been used to give continued movement to certain toys, usually a matter of falling weights. The "Bowler Andy Mill" made by the Wolverine Supply & Manufacturing Co. of the United States c.1914 is powered by metal balls rolling, one at a time, from a hopper at the top of a tower into a hoist. The weight of each ball causes the hoist to descend rapidly when the ball is ejected. A counterweight raises the hoist immediately to collect the next ball. The rising and falling of the hoist causes a "windmill" to revolve on top of the tower. "Sandy Andy" is another Wolverine toy from the same period. Here the power is supplied by sand running from a hopper. An open counterweighted truck at the top of a gradient fills with sand until it is heavy enough to overcome the

ABOVE LEFT

Maker **Schuco (Schreyer & Co.)**

Marks *Schuco*

Date **1930s**

Length **3¾in (9.5cm)**

This Schuco "Roller" from the 1930s is fitted with a fly-wheel mechanism. Some models were fitted with a single wing in front of the steering wheel and given a "human" pilot, thus turning the toy into a simple representation of a flying machine. The Schuco "Rollers" are harder to find than many of the company's novelty clockwork figures.

ABOVE RIGHT

Maker **Wolverine Supply & Manufacturing Co.**

Marks *Wolverine Supply & Mfg Co.*

Date **1930s**

Width **7¾in (20cm)**

This musical automaton picks out a tune on the xylophone directed by the specially designed, interchangeable cams such as the one in the foreground. To change the melody, simply change the cam! This clockwork toy is known as the "Zilotone" and was a product of the U.S. Wolverine Supply & Manufacturing Co. Examples of this toy do keep turning up – but they are expensive! *Sotheby's*

ABOVE

Maker **Wells**

Marks **None**

Date **1930s**

Length **14in (36cm)**

These tinplate lorries – a searchlight lorry (*left*) and an anti-aircraft gun lorry (*right*) – were rather crudely produced. The gun was

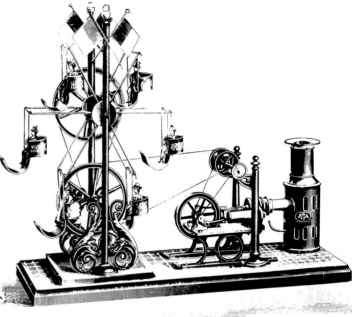

This type of toy was produced by various German toy makers. Most were designed to be operated either by winding a hand-wheel or via a belt-drive from a model stationary steam engine. The toy illustrated has its own clockwork mechanism installed within the blacksmith's anvil. A flint mechanism adds to the realism by providing sparks as the hammer strikes. An early catalogue of the Nuremberg firm Doll & Cie. shows a very similar figure operated by hand and with the anvil replaced by the stump of a tree. Such toys are, in general, reasonably easy to find.

An exotic carousel powered by a hot air engine, made by Plank in the early 1900s.

designed to fire "caps" and the searchlight could be worked by battery – indeed, both models were fitted with electric headlamps powered from a battery slung beneath the chassis. Practically unsaleable a few years ago, these are good examples of toys that are now becoming increasingly hard to find and are being collected more for their curiosity value than for the quality of the construction or design.

Chester Toy and Doll Museum

Maker **Märklin**
Marks *G.M. & Cie.* [intertwined] in a shield
Date **1906**
This is a most unusual and ingenious gauge I railway truck. It is a model of a heating wagon of the type in use at the beginning of this century. A spirit burner is used to heat water inside the truck, and the hot water circulates through a system of pipes to the adjoining carriages. This is very rare.

pull of the counterweight. It runs down the slope, empties itself, and is then pulled back for more. These toys are not over popular among collectors – perhaps they would be more suitable as "executive toys".

Clockwork, however, has always been the favourite form of power source for automata and toy makers. In the 1880s Ernst Paul Lehmann introduced the simple coiled "piano-wire" spring mechanism, a device later adopted by other toy makers. Attempts to use electric motors as power sources for toys met with little success in cars and boats, but they proved to be ideal for toy railways, eventually replacing clockwork altogether. In the 1950s Japanese toy manufacturers produced a vast range of novelty toys activated by small battery-powered electric motors. The declining German toy industry produced very few battery-powered toys at that particular period, although Schuco included a range of battery-operated cars and airliners in its catalogue.

Germany was definitely the world leader in toy production from the early days to the end of the 1930s. The toys produced there were invariably of a high standard of quality and excellent value for money within a wide price range. Theodore F. Märklin founded the most famous of all German toy-making firms in 1859 at Göppingen. Märklin originally manufactured a variety of small toys, including children's toy cooking ranges. With the passing of time the firm expanded and turned out a large variety of wonderfully made toys, including ships, trains and novelties. Before World War I it also manufactured Meccano, the British construction outfit, under licence. The early toys by Märklin are keenly sought after by collectors today all over the world, and by German collectors in particular.

Other famous German firms included Bing, at one time the country's leading toy manufacturer: it had annual sales of around 27 million

Deutschmarks in 1928. The trade depression that resulted in the Wall Street Crash in the following year proved also to be a disaster for Bing, and eventually led to the firm's being taken over by the rival manufacturer Karl Bub.

Because most of the German toymakers were to be found in the area around Nuremberg, the city became an important centre for toy marketing. Indeed, even though Nuremberg's toy-making image is long gone, it is still the regular venue for an important international toy trade fair.

In France the toy, doll and automata industry grew up in Paris with, in the early days, outworkers being employed to make parts from metal, which, as in Germany, they had often foraged from rubbish dumps. Like

Maker **Unknown Japanese**
Marks **None**
Date **1960s**
Height (centre) 5in (13cm); (left- and right-hand) 8in (21cm)

Three colourful novelty tinplate automata from Japan. The figure in the centre "plays" a xylophone, while the other two figures tap-dance. All three are clockwork. Amusing small toys such as these are quite desirable. Colourful and well made, they take up little room in the home and make excellent "talking pieces". Unfortunately, they are fairly hard to find.

Maker **Possibly unknown French**
Marks **None**
Date *c.*1950
Length **7½in (19cm)**

A hand-enamelled toy pigeon with a clockwork mechanism, which may have been made in France but could well have come from Germany. There are no identification marks, and many toys were produced in this style on the Continent during the early years of this century. The bird travels forwards with typical head movements. These toys are seen occasionally on toy stalls and in auctions.

OPPOSITE
A pageful of novelty toys from the very wide selection produced by the Nuremberg company Emil Hausmann in the late 1920s.

their German equivalents, they lived and worked hard in poor conditions for little reward.

Many interesting tinplate toys came from the French manufacturers, especially from the factory of Fernand Martin. From boyhood Martin had been fascinated by engineering, and by 1880 his factory on the Boulevard de Menilmontant in Paris employed over 200 workers who were turning out some 8,000 mechanical toy figures each year up to the outbreak of World War I. These figures walked, performed acrobatic tricks and one even played a piano. Many of the toys were simply powered by elastic drive; others had clockwork mechanisms.

The toy manufacturers of the United States developed a different style in their toy making from their European counterparts. In the mid-19th century the companies of Ives and George W. Brown & Co. were producing a very wide range of playthings, including hand-painted horse-drawn trams and locomotives. Ives quickly introduced a selection of attractive mechanically powered tinplate toys. At the same time Althof, Bergmann & Co. was offering a range of attractive clockwork toys, including a novel "hoop toy", whose clockwork motor caused a mechanical figure to trundle a hoop forwards.

In the United Kingdom the toy industry was not quite so well developed. The most important toy-making firm was the Meccano Company of Liverpool, founded in 1901 by Frank Hornby to manufacture his famous metal-strip constructional outfits. The equally popular range

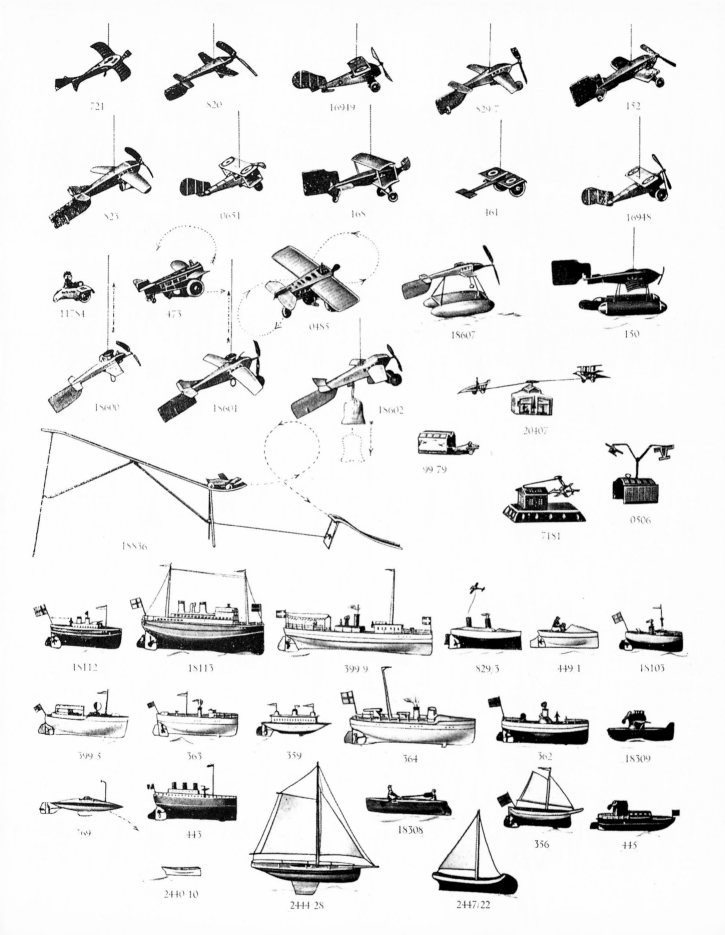

721 820 16949 829 7 152

823 0651 168 461 16948

11784 473 0485 18607 150

18600 18601 18602 20407

9979 18836 7181 0506

18112 18113 399 9 829/3 449 1 18103

399 5 363 359 364 362 18309

769 443 18308 356 445

2440 10 2444 28 2447/22

ABOVE
Maker   **Cardini**
Marks   **None**
Date   *c.*1925
Diameter   **19in (48cm)**
Two carousel toys by the Italian toy maker
Cardini. The original cardboard boxes of
both toys are designed to form the
appropriately decorated bases to hold the
tinplate "rides". These interesting toys are
not often found for sale. *Sotheby's*

Maker **Unknown Japanese**
Marks *W.U.* [in a diamond] *Made in Japan*
Date **1930s**
Height **10½in (27cm)**
This pre-war Japanese clockwork drummer boy has a tinplate body and celluloid head. A rare example of an early Japanese toy.

OPPOSITE
Maker **Burnett Ltd**
Marks [St George and the dragon
trademark] *Made in England*
Date **c.1910**
Length **7in (18cm)**
This early tinplate armoured car with gunner is a simple but pleasing clockwork toy made by Burnett, the British company that was eventually taken over by Chad Valley. Burnett Ltd had moved to London by 1914; before then the company's address had been Birmingham, and the trademark on this toy suggests that it was made in Birmingham, obviously well before the outbreak of World War I. Hard to find, although examples do turn up occasionally.

of Hornby trains followed in the 1920s and 1930s, and branches were opened in France and the United States to serve local tastes. The well-known diecast Dinky Toys were also produced by the factory.

Tinplate toys were manufactured in Britain by Burnett and Chad Valley, the latter firm eventually taking over the former. Wells Brimtoy was originally two separate firms, Brimtoy having specialized in a cheap line of tinplate train sets. Bassett-Lowke produced a range of well-made model railway items and also commissioned, among others, the German firm of Bing to provide models. The American firm of Marx made tin toys in Britain, first at its factory in Dudley in the Midlands and later in Wales.

Some very appealing tin toys were made in Italy and Spain, although they were not too well known except in their countries of origin.

3.
WHAT TO COLLECT

So many types of tin toys have been produced by such a wide range of manufacturers that it would be almost impossible to collect an example of each type of toy or an example of each manufacturer's output. Most collectors instead prefer to concentrate on one kind of toy or, less often, on the products of a single manufacturer. Among the most popular subjects for collection are, of course, trains, road vehicles and boats, but aircraft and novelty toys also form the basis of many collections. Other collectors choose character toys, battery toys or robots and space toys, while yet others select penny toys. Whatever your own preference, you should still be able to find items for sale at auctions or swap meets that will allow you to build up a specialist collection of the type of toy that especially appeals to you.

TOY TRAINS

The Steam Age heralded a new and wonderful era for man and allowed people to travel about and transport goods at speeds never before experienced. Toy manufacturers were quick to appreciate the possibili-

OPPOSITE
Maker **Unknown**
Marks **None on toy; box labelled** *Hall's Patent Whistling Railway Engine. Made in Germany*
Date **Late 19th century**
Length 10½in (27cm)

"Hall's Patent Whistling Railway Engine" is an early German carpet toy. It seems that no examples of these toys that actually work have survived, but the theory is that, by running the toy backwards for a short distance, the mechanism is wound up for the forward run, the train whistling as it goes.

The engine illustrated here has survived with its rare original box, and it is shown together with a photograph of the Scottish boy who received the train as a gift on 1 January 1889. His name was Daniel Fisher McCallum, and he was photographed with his sister. This toy turns up at auctions from time to time, but finding it with its box is extremely difficult.

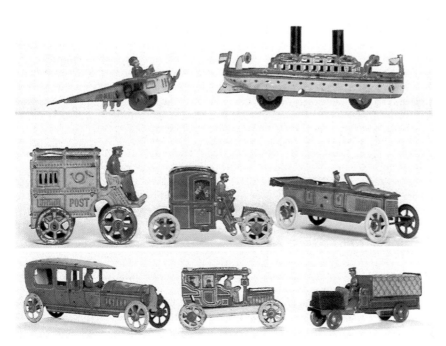

A selection of penny toys. Although these cheap little toys were manufactured in many countries, the best range came from Germany, where toy makers produced some excellently lithographed examples that are works of art in their own right. Penny toys vary in availability, although they are generally hard to come by – especially the German-made examples, which are more desirable. *Sotheby's*

ties of this marvellous new form of travel along specially laid "rail roads", and the toy train was to become perhaps the most popular of all toys – a plaything that had the double advantage of appealing to fathers as well as their sons.

The first model locomotives were designed from the educational point of view. They were simple steam-powered devices, which tended to leak boiling water over the carpet as they puffed along, thereby earning their nickname of "dribblers". Made of brass, they appeared on sale in shops specializing in scientific instruments and were classed as "scientific toys". Several British companies produced "dribblers", among them the London-based Stevens's Model Dockyard, Newton & Co., John Theobald, J. Bateman & Co. and Lucas & Davies, and Clyde Model Dockyard, Glasgow, H. Wiles, Manchester, and British Modelling & Electric Co. of Leek, Staffordshire. In France, Radiguet & Massiot are known to have manufactured "dribblers".

Gradually other types of train were introduced by different manufacturers, and tinplate took over from brass and clockwork while electric motors were used to provide the motive power. Some toy trains had no means of propulsion and were meant to be pushed along or pulled by a string, like the enchantingly naïve productions of the German firms of Lutz (a maker of high quality toys which was later absorbed by Märklin) and Fischer. These are referred to as "carpet toys" or "floor trains" because they had no track to run on, although a few of these trackless locomotives incorporated clockwork mechanisms. Many early French trains had no rails, and manufacturers included Charles Rossignol, F.V. (Faivre or Favre) and Maltête & Parent.

Some of the early model locomotives were reasonable representations of their real-life counterparts, others were not and there was no definite period when each type existed, as one firm could be producing carpet toys at the same time as it was marketing clockwork-powered train sets.

One curious carpet toy that appeared in the 1880s was advertised as "Hall's Patent Whistling Engine" – it whistled realistically as it was propelled forward by its mechanism. Although it *looks* as if it was of German manufacture, it is generally believed to have been of English make. However, this particular toy came in a cardboard box clearly labelled "Made in Germany", and it has been suggested that it could have been produced by Schoenner. The box label also states "The Mechanism guaranteed of Steel (no Elastic used)", and the instructions, printed in German, French and English, continue: "Wind the engine by turning backwards the handle connected with the right hand hind wheel until brought to a stop (about 7 turns); then before releasing the handle turn the brake between the spokes of the wheel. Place the engine on the ground and start it by moving inwards the lever handle at the back." None of the surviving examples I have seen ever seem to work, and the mechanism cannot be examined without disassembling the toy.

Penny toy type trains – simple, but often quite attractive miniatures – appeared on the market from German and French toy makers. Their

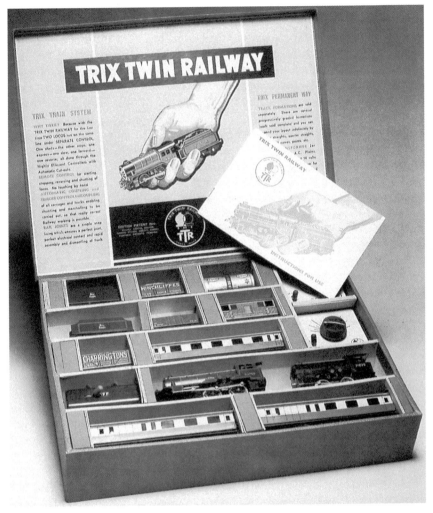

Maker **Trix**
Marks *T.T.R.*
Date **1950s**
Length **3–4in (7–10cm) average**

After World War II the popularity of gauge O scale model railways gave way to the smaller HO and OO gauges introduced in the 1930s. Frank Hornby, of Meccano and Dinky Toy fame, developed the neat "Dublo" range using, at first, 3-rail track but later providing a more realistic 2–rail track.

The Trix organization originated in Germany, where it had taken over the old Distler factory, but production later moved to Britain. The Trix Twin Railway was noted for the fact that two locomotives could be independently operated on the same electric track. The photograph shows one of the number of Trix Twin Railway outfits to appear during the 1950s, this particular model containing two locomotives – a "Hunt" class engine for the passenger coaches and a tank locomotive to pull the goods wagons. Strictly speaking, the locomotives are not "tin toys", being of diecast metal, but the rolling stock is of tinplate construction. German collectors tend to prefer the German-made Trix models.

larger clockwork counterparts were introduced in the early years of the second half of the 19th century, and toy trains that actually ran along tinplate tracks came later. Manufacturers initially found it difficult to design models that would run on track like the real thing, but the problems were overcome later in the century and tracks of a variety of gauges were produced. However, it was not until 1891 that the German firm of Märklin attempted to standardize track width and led to the introduction of the popular gauge O. Several other gauges were still available, but gauge O – 35mm between the rails – proved to be the favourite. Märklin designed useful sectional track and incorporated crossings and points to add to the realism of the lay-outs. The company also pioneered the introduction of track accessories including tinplate stations, locomotive sheds, signals, standard lamps, cranes and tunnels.

Gauge O track was introduced to America by Ives of Bridgeport, one of the country's top toy makers, and other countries likewise accepted this favourite gauge, realizing that such standardization would be a great asset as they increasingly turned to mass production. Larger gauges were popular, too, especially for the more spacious garden lay-outs. The trend to smaller gauges came during the late 1930s, when the demand arose for more compact, scenic lay-outs. Leaders in the smaller OO and HO gauges were the German firm of Trix and the British firm of Meccano, which introduced the Hornby Dublo system in 1938.

Earlier, in 1921, the German company Bing brought out its "Miniature Table Railway", an idea it had first considered just before World War I. These delightfully lithographed models – many in the liveries of British railway companies – came in attractively boxed sets complete with rolling stock, track and accessories, which could include signals, signal-box, tunnel, level-crossing and station, according to the price of the boxed set. The first locomotives were driven by clockwork, and electric versions were available by 1925. This series was continued by the firm of Karl Bub after its take over of Bing in 1933. The scale of 1:76 chosen for this toy was also used for the later Hornby Dublo system, but it proved unpopular with model railway enthusiasts who sought realism in their lay-outs.

There is a clear division between toy train collectors and modellers. The former are not too worried about realism, seeing a toy train set as something of an appealing novelty. The railway modeller is, on the other hand, a stickler for detail and a true railway enthusiast who takes his interest seriously, and we must leave his kind to the many specialist books that deal with accurate scale modelling and turn our attention instead in the direction of the mass-produced tin toy.

Take the products of Frank Hornby, for instance – the famous Hornby trains, which certainly represent the very best of British tinplate toys. Here we have a little mystery: was the first Hornby train a German product? The firm's early catalogues illustrate a range of an 0-4-0* tank engine, which, along with its accompanying tender and carriages, certainly has a Germanic appearance. One of these engines is named *George the Fifth*, presumably after the prototype of that name which is known to have existed just before World War I.

It is known that Meccano had links with Märklin, which provided some of the accessories incorporated in the famous metal-strip construction toy, so there is no need to dismiss the idea that there was no business association with Bing. Although some Hornby enthusiasts appreciate this and a few are willing to admit to some kind of German connection, there are many who do not subscribe to this theory.

However, this particular Hornby 0-4-0 is almost exactly like the 0-4-0 clockwork tank engine and rolling stock sold by Bing just before the

*In the U.K. locomotives are usually described by the Whyte system of classification by which the first figure indicates the number of leading wheels, the second figure the number of driving wheels and the third figure the number of trailing wheels.

outbreak of World War I – that company even issued a black version named *George the Fifth*.

Basing his theory on information from ex-Meccano employees, the late Rikki Thompson of Manchester, believed that the materials were sent over from Germany to the Liverpool factory for assembly there. The outbreak of war interrupted production and, when peace was restored, the factory introduced its new "nut and bolted" locomotives using the clockwork motors intended for the *George the Fifth* engines. Later, when anti-German feelings had subsided, the remaining Bing locomotives were assembled and given new clockwork mechanisms made by Maccano. It is interesting to note that, unlike there original German counterparts, these later engines had no reverse gearing. These locomotives appear in the *Hornby Book of Trains* for 1925 (there is no reference to them in later editions) as *George the Fifth*; they were also available in the liveries of the Midland Railway and the Great Northern Railway.

Although Hornby may be the best known of the British companies manufacturing small gauge toy trains, the products of Brimtoy, Chad Valley, Whitanco and Wells are also of interest even if they are not of such good quality.

The other important British manufacturer and distributor of toy trains was Bassett-Lowke, a Northampton company founded in 1899 by Wenmann J. Bassett-Lowke. A major importer of the products of such German companies as Bing and Carette into Britain, Bassett-Lowke offered a wide range of both gauges and models for sale through his mail order catalogues. The German-made trains, in the liveries of all the

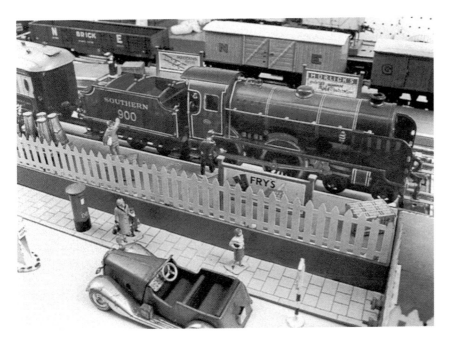

A realistic gauge O model railway layout with rolling stock and a 4-4-0 "Eton" locomotive and tender in Southern Railway livery. The locomotive dates from the 1930s, as does the Tri-ang Minic open tourer (carrying "L" plates) in the foreground. A rare Hornby product such as this "Eton" locomotive in good condition would be keenly collected.

Courtesy Vintage Toy & Train Museum, Sidmouth, Devon

Maker **Bing**
Marks *BW* [in Bing cypher]
Date **1920s**
Length **(locomotive) 14in (36cm)**

A sturdy 4-4-0 live-steam locomotive and tender made in gauge O by Gebrüder Bing of Nuremberg. Named the *Black Prince*, this model was produced in various gauges, and it was popular in Britain where it was marketed by Bassett-Lowke. Some examples were fitted with powerful clockwork mechanisms, but the locomotive shown here is a steam-powered version, which, to judge from the small amount of paint blistering from the burner, has obviously been little used. The methylated spirit fuel was stored in the tender and reached the burner under the boiler by way of a rubber connecting tube. The locomotive was marketed throughout the 1920s. Examples such as this can be found – with difficulty – but the condition can vary considerably.

British railway companies and designed to resemble their British prototypes, that Bassett-Lowke marketed in Britain are among the most sought-after of all toy trains by British collectors.

The products of the German firm Märklin are among the finest – indeed, many would say *the* finest – of all toy trains. Nowadays they are highly sought after by collectors, particularly in Germany, where Märklin items are held in the highest esteem. Over the years Märklin's output was prodigious, although it has to be admitted that, while the quality of its products was first class among mass-produced toys, the company's railway outlines were not often noted for the accuracy of their modelling. The charm of Märklin products – including the non-railway toys – lies in their ingenuity and beautiful workmanship.

Many excellent models in a variety of gauges came from the other great German toy-making firms – Bing, Bub, Issmayer, Schoenner, Fleischmann, Günthermann, Carette, Distler, for example. Their products

varied in appeal; Karl Bub, for instance, included in its range gauge I locomotives designed to run on gauge O track, a somewhat unwieldy alliance that was not overly popular originally, although the passage of time has given these trains a charm of their own for toy collectors today.

German toy train manufacturers went to great lengths to model the trains destined for Britain on the prototypes in service there, Bing's products in particular achieving a remarkable degree of realism. After Bassett-Lowke, one of the other main outlets for German toy trains was the London store Gamage's, which showed the products of many German companies, including Märklin, Carette and Bing, in its catalogues and distributed the trains not only throughout Britain but also throughout the then far-flung British Empire.

German toy manufacturers also regarded the United States as a prime export target, and many American outline locomotives – and many more European outline locomotives "Americanized" by the addition of cow-catcher and bell – were exported across the Atlantic. There they encountered strong competition from Ives, which had started making toy locomotives from cast-iron before, in the early 1900s, beginning to manufacture tinplate models, many of which were copies of toys already being made in Germany. More opposition to the German invasion of the American market came from such firms as Lionel and American Flyer, which were supplying toys that could be manufactured efficiently at very competitive prices.

French toy railways appeared in the 1870s. As we have seen, the first were in the tradition of the "scientific toy" and followed the "dribbler"

Tinplate model-railway accessories have a fascination all their own. This photograph shows just a few of the kind of trackside items that were manufactured by toy makers throughout Europe and America, with German firms leading the way. Most of the accessories were made to match the scale of the popular gauge O and gauge I. Such toys vary considerably in their degree of rarity, their value largely depending on the manufacturer or their age. *Sotheby's*

Maker **Richard & Co.**
Marks *Ri [dancing man] Co of Bavaria*
      printed on rear of vehicle
Date **1930s**
Length **9½in (24cm)**

The ancient frame aerial dates this "radio car" with its four members of the police flying squad to the 1920s and the arrival of the "wireless". The car still carries its original label, indicating that it had been distributed to the trade by the Moses Kohnstam organization, which traded as Moko. Labels like the one dangling from the windscreen and other surviving examples of the original packing – instruction leaflets, guarantee slips and, above all, the original boxes – add greatly to the interest (and therefore the value) of a toy.

This particular toy is fitted with working searchlights on its bonnet, which are powered from a battery slung beneath the chassis and geared to the mechanism to give a scanning movement. Objects such as this searchlight detract from any realism the toy may otherwise possess but, because they are designed as playthings, work wonders with the imaginative minds of the children for whom they were intended. This toy is rare. *Chester Toy and Doll Museum*

styles of Britain and Germany. Towards the end of the 19th century a firm by the name of Brianne manufactured some interesting railway accessories for the German trains it was importing into France. One of its products was a fascinating representation of the Gare du Nord in Paris, complete with decorative statuettes on the roof. The firm is also known to have produced a large train, powered by electricity, designed for an outdoor track.

J.E.P. (Jouets de Paris) was the most prolific toy train manufacturer in France. The company offered a variety of products over the years, powered by both electric and clockwork motors. In 1925 it produced trains in HO scale, again in clockwork and electric, with lithographed tinplate bodies. Rossignol was another French firm famous for its economically priced, colourful tinplate toys. The firm's products were solely produced as toys, with little attempt being made to manufacture models of the real thing. They were purely carpet toys, made for the amusement of uncritical children.

ROAD VEHICLES

Automotive toys appeal to collectors who like to display models of their favourite motor cars, lorries, vans and buses in their showcases. Throughout the years many toys have been manufactured to reflect the history of the "horseless carriage" in all its variations, and surviving examples of the early products today realize very high prices at auctions.

MOTOR CARS

The early toy motor vehicles were extremely well produced from hand-soldered parts and finished by hand enamelling. Before 1914 toy cars included quite excellently detailed models of the original Mercedes, De Dion or whatever contemporary car they were intended to represent. Again, the majority of the best examples were made by the German firms

Karl Bub produced this interesting motor car in the 1920s. Its clockwork motor had a reverse gear, it was fitted with two spare wheels, and the windows were glazed. At 17¼in (44cm) long, it was an impressive toy.

Maker **Günthermann**
Length **11¾in (30cm)**
Another fine Günthermann toy in the style of an early racing car competing in the Gordon Bennett Cup Motor Race. There should be two figures representing the speeding drivers, but they are missing from this model. Hidden bellows, powered by the clockwork, sound a warning horn when the car is in motion. Note the chain drive to the rear, rubber-tyred wheels. With or without the figures, this is very rare.

Maker **Hess**
Marks *J.L.H.* monogram
Length **8¾in (22cm)**

The firm of Mattheus Hess was one of Germany's longest-established toy-making concerns. It tended to favour fly-wheel mechanisms, hand-cranked by a winding handle protruding from the radiator, as the means of propulsion for many of its toy vehicles. The illustration shows an early example of this type of toy, styled after the racing cars of the period, and it is possible to see how the spinning inertia mechanism transferred its power to one of the front wheels. Such toys are rare.

of Bing, Märklin and Carette. The toy vehicles of another Nuremberg company, Günthermann, are also extremely collectable, especially its series of Gordon Bennett racing cars. Founded in 1877, the company produced its first car in 1898 and included in its range of good quality toy cars, limousines, saloons and even convertibles.

Some of these early toys may not have been designed to represent any particular make of car, but they were all generally fitted with opening doors and realistic accessories – some even had miniature working oil-lamps. Most models were powered by clockwork, were capable of being put into reverse gear and had a working handbrake. The windows would probably have the luxury of being glazed with bevelled glass, and the wheels fitted with solid rubber tyres. Some models were even powered by a small steam plant.

One of the earliest of the Nuremberg toy manufacturers was the company founded in 1826 by Mattheus Hess. Noted for their fine

Maker **Hess**
Marks **Gothic *H* in a shield**
Date *c.* 1898
Length 8¾in (22cm)

This model, an early item from Hess, is a wonderful toy, evocative of the early days of motoring. Beautifully designed and lithographed, the figures add to the realism. Powered by Hess's preferred inertia mechanism, it is very rare.

Maker **Lehmann**
Marks *Lehmann*
Date **1900–35**
Length 4¾in (12cm)

Lehmann manufactured a wide range of novelty toys, most appearing between 1918 and 1939. This toy is typical of the company's output: it is well made and has an amusing action. The baker or pretzel vendor is pestered by a mischievous chimney sweep as he pedals his tricycle truck. On the cart is a bell which rings as the truck trundles along. A rare toy.

RIGHT
Maker **Lehmann**
Marks *EPL* [in bell] *Marke Lehmann*
Date **1906–16**
Length **8¾in (22cm)**

One of the simpler novelties from the Lehmann factory, "Oho" has no fancy actions: wind it up and it travels forwards or in circles, according to the way the adjustable steering is set. This was a particularly popular toy when it first appeared. It is now quite a collectable item and a "must" for anyone collecting Lehmann toys. It is not as rare as some of the company's other toys.

The Schuco (Schreyer & Co.) "Studio" was an immensely popular toy during the 1930s. Designed to represent a famous contemporary Mercedes racing car, it had a clockwork motor that could be wound up either with a key or by pressing the car down on its springs and drawing it backwards. The car came complete with a set of tools to remove the wheels and tyres, and it could be steered by turning the steering wheel. The rear wheels were driven through differential gears.

Although the firm of Schuco no longer exists, this model has been re-introduced by Gama (Mangold) and sold under the Schuco trademark together with some reproductions of the Schuco "Old Timer" series of the 1960s.

decoration, Hess toy cars are remarkable for the flywheel mechanisms used to power them. Production ended in 1934, and Hess toy cars are extremely desirable today. Among the beautifully lithographed cars are two-seaters, four-seaters and racing cars, all the "Hessmobils" being propelled by a flywheel.

Other notable German toy car manufacturers were Lehmann (founded in Brandenburg in 1881), Tipp & Co. (whose cars are marked *TCO* on the bonnets) and Bub (whose finely lithographed cars often had metal wheels).

Fine model cars also emerged from France. J.E.P. (which had been founded in 1899 when it was known as the Société Industrielle de Ferblanterie) generally put the trademark of the toy's prototype on the radiator of its products. Citroën toy cars were made to resemble as closely as possible the original cars of that name: they often had opening doors and windows, and some even had working lights. Produced from 1923, they were trademarked with a stencilled motif incorporating the name André Citroën. Rossignol, which was founded in 1868, is believed to have made a model car earlier than any of the German toy companies. Whether this is true or not, Rossignol certainly produced an attractive range of toy cars, including representations of Renaults and Peugeots.

In Italy toy cars were produced by the Omegna company Cardini, whose products bore the company crest while the wheels were marked "Pirelli-cord". Most of its cars were rather small, although they were beautifully finished. The boxes in which they were packaged were designed to be converted into miniature garages.

American manufacturers seemed on the whole to prefer sheet-metal,

diecast or cast-iron model vehicles and produced very little in tinplate, although both Marx and Kingsbury used tinplate for some of their lines. Kingsbury was responsible for a large model of the British racing car *Bluebird*, and Marx made a fascinating novelty car known as the "Amos and Andy Fresh Air Cab". This had an amusing action, but did not represent a specific make of car. "Leaping Lena" was another well-known American novelty car with an action that resembled a bucking bronco. It was made in the 1920s and 1930s by Strauss, a company eventually taken over by Marx.

Tinplate cars appeared over the years in all shapes and sizes, echoing the changing fashions all along. Some fine construction outfits of cars were marketed by both Märklin and by Meccano. These were sold in decorative boxes with all the components ready for assembly, using nuts and bolts to fasten them together. The British firm of Chad Valley produced a range of "Ubilda" models, including a motor car and a fire-engine. ("Ubilda" was a trademark of Burnett, a firm taken over by Chad Valley.) They were excellent tin toys but of an inferior quality to the Märklin and Meccano products.

Many novelty models, operated by a variety of ingenious actions, were marketed, and one of the leading manufacturers in this field was Schreyer & Co. – best known by its tradename Schuco. Founded in Nuremberg in 1912 by Schreyer and Müller, Schuco produced a range of cleverly constructed sports cars. The "Steerable Driving School Car", which bore a passing resemblance to a Mercedes racing car, was provided with a starting crank, differential gears, rack and pinion steering and changeable tyres; the "Turn Back" car was guaranteed not to fall off tables.

Maker **Tipp & Co.**
Marks *TCO monogram*
Date **1920s–1930s**
Length **15¾in (40cm)**
A German-made car resembling a Rolls Royce but with a bull dog as the mascot. The passenger doors open realistically, and the steering can be adjusted. The driver is typical of Tipp cars of this period. This car is rare.

RIGHT

Maker **Tomiyama**

Marks *Tomiyama* and stylized Teddy Bear's head

Date **Early 1960s**

Length **16in (41cm)**

Japanese ingenuity is displayed in the actions of this model racing-car, the "Firebird Race Car", which is battery powered. When it is switched on the engine starts to run and lights flash through the transparent red panel on the bonnet. The car pulls away, circles around for a while and then stops. The driver raises his right arm a couple of times in a "pit-stop" signal, revs up the engine and pulls away again. The sequence is repeated. These toys can be difficult to find if you are looking for one to complete a collection, but they do turn up.

OPPOSITE ABOVE

Maker **Bandai**

Marks **Gothic** *B* in a *C*

Date **1950–60**

Length **12in (31cm)**

These beautifully made tinplate automobiles are examples of some of the fine models that were made in Japan during the 1950s and 1960s. Both are the products of Bandai, a firm noted for the excellence of its toys – the Rolls Royce "Silver Cloud" (*left*) has a friction-drive, while the Ferrari is battery powered and has working headlights, horn and gears. Such toys in good condition are in great demand by collectors today, especially the models of 1950s and '60s American limousines.

OPPOSITE BELOW

Maker **Masutoku Toy Factory**

Marks *M.T.* [in a diamond] *Japan*

Date **1950s–1960s**

Length **9in (23cm)**

A fantasy car from Japan, this battery toy has coloured balls that jump up and down in the transparent cylinders on the bonnet and a driver who constantly raises his hat as he drives along. The car is obviously well travelled, for souvenir labels from various places in the U.S.A. are plastered over the sides. These toys turn up from time to time in auction sales and at toy fairs. Their appeal lies in their comical actions and design and in the excellence of the manufacture.

Until 1939 clockwork remained the favourite form of propulsion, with friction drive a close second. After World War II, however, when the world's toy market began to be dominated by Japan, there was a move to battery-operated vehicles. Japanese-made cars of the 1960s, some produced in imitation of the contemporary, rather opulent American style, are now very collectable. Today's collectors tend to favour not one manufacturer but one type of car – Cadillac, Plymouth, Buick and so forth. Most major Japanese companies offered these beautifully made cars, including Alps, Bandai, Taiyo and Ichiko. Many of these tinplate, battery-powered cars had working lights and horns, and some had working shift gears, opening bonnets and boots (trunks) and even working windscreeen wipers.

Among British products tinplate vehicles from the Tri-ang "Minic" range form an ideal subject for collection and are still relatively easy to find at reasonable prices. It was in the 1930s that Lines Brothers, under its Tri-ang trademark, started to produce, from its south London factory, a range of small road vehicles in the "Minic" series. These vehicles were designed to a scale sufficiently accurate to allow them to be incorporated in the popular gauge O toy railway lay-outs of the day, and they helped to add extra realism and interest to the display.

The models, which enjoyed great popularity for many years, represented contemporary cars, vans, lorries and other road vehicles (including a London taxicab), as well as a few military items. They were extremely well made and finished and were powered by clockwork. Some of them vaguely resembled known makes of the real thing – Rolls Royce and Vauxhall cars in particular – but were near enough to please the young boys at whom the range was aimed.

Tri-ang issued some of the toys in boxed presentation sets, and in 1936 it introduced a construction outfit from which six vehicles could be built

Maker **Lines Brothers**
Marks *Tri-ang Minic Toys. Made in England*
Date **Late 1930s**
Length **4½in (11cm) average**
The popularity of gauge O railways encouraged Lines Brothers to introduce a series of small-scale tinplate road vehicles, which could be used to add extra realism to model-railway layouts. The three limousines illustrated here vaguely represent the type of better-class automobile seen on British roads during the 1930s. They have clockwork motors, and their manufacture was resumed after World War II. Friction mechanisms were introduced later, and eventually the last of the Minics were produced from plastic. The Tri-ang range included all kinds of road vehicles, from lorries to buses and even military vehicles. Availability varies according to model, but there is still time to start a collection!

– a tractor, a cabriolet, a limousine, a streamlined saloon, a delivery lorry and a transport van. All the parts were ready for assembly – for which tools were supplied – and were chromium-plated where necessary. The bodywork was left for the owner to colour using the paints included in the well-made oak cabinet in which the set was sold. It was quite an expensive outfit and, although it was advertised as the "Construction Set No. 1", no more versions appeared.

Tri-ang ceased production in the early 1940s and the factory was turned over to essential war work. However, in 1945 production was resumed and "Minic" toys continued to be made well into the 1960s, although plastic models were gradually introduced into the range. Some models also were fitted with flywheel drive instead of clockwork.

"Minic" toys are an ideal subject for specialization. They are still to be found, and their prices are reasonably low compared with those of many of their counterparts produced during the same period. The signs are, however, that they will soon be the subject of increased attention from collectors. The neat toy vehicles produced in the late 1970s by Kellermann would also build into a fine specialist collection. Kellermann, another Nuremberg company, was founded c.1910. Its friction-drive,

Dinky-sized models were flawlessly pressed in intricate detail so excellent that, at first glance, they could easily be mistaken for quality diecast toys.

COMMERCIAL VEHICLES

Trucks, vans, and other commercial vehicles have also been manufactured in miniature, and the range includes a wide selection of tinplate versions of steam lorries and traction engines. Some of these were decorated with contemporary trade advertising and logos, features that add extra nostalgic interest to any toy commercial vehicle, and are guaranteed to offer extra appeal to collectors.

Fire-engines make an interesting subject for collection, as do ambulances, post-office vehicles and so on. Some collectors specialize in just one type of road vehicle, often extending their search into the realms of diecast and plastic toys. Military vehicles of all kinds, including tanks, also often form part of specialist collections. They have appeared across the years, with the most ingenious examples hailing from Germany.

MOTOR CYCLES

Motor cycles are another excellent subject for building a collection, and

Delivery van
Maker **Unknown**
Marks *Huntley & Palmers* **but no maker's marks**
Date **Late 1920s to early 1930s**
Length **7¾in (20cm)**

Locomotive
Maker **Unknown**
Marks *William Crawford & Sons Ltd* **but no maker's marks**
Date **Late 1920s to early 1930s**
Length **7¾in (20cm)**

Of the two novelty biscuit tins, the delivery van was obviously used to market the products of Messrs. Huntley & Palmers, but the rarer of the two is the one in the form of a tank locomotive in the blue livery of the Caledonian Railway and issued by William Crawford & Sons Ltd. Novelty containers such as these represent the skills of various tinplate manufacturers, some of which still exist as part of the Metal Box Co. The specialized interest in these novelty biscuit tins that has grown up in recent years has forced up prices and turned the majority of them into scarce items.

The 1959 Tipp & Co. catalogue contained this illustration of a motor scooter and rider. As the catalogue reveals: " 'Bella' motor scooter travels automatically in a square with the rider signalling each change of direction by lifting his left arm and turning his head." The prototype of "Bella" was made by the German motorcycle firm Zundapp as an answer to the contemporary Italian Vespa and Lambretta scooters.

ABOVE
Maker **Tipp & Co.**
Marks *TCO* **monogram**
Date **Late 1950s–early 1960s**
Length **8in (21cm)**
This fine tinplate model of a Zundapp "Bella" motor scooter hails, like the original, from West Germany. A well-engineered production from Tipp & Co., the clockwork-powered mechanism also causes the driver to raise his arm to signal a left turn. A similar model was produced without this action, and although both are quite rare, the animated version is much harder to find.

RIGHT
Maker **Victor Bonnet et Cie.**
Marks *Vébé*
Date **1920s**
Length **12in (31cm)**
This clockwork vehicle is one of a series made by the French company of Victor Bonnet et Cie. These toys were particularly well produced, and this example is illustrated with the lid of its original box. The company's trademark "V.B. et Cie." may be seen on the lid, together with the trademark of Fernand Martin of Paris; Martin was taken over by Bonnet in the 1920s. Although not particularly rare, these are difficult toys to find. *Chester Toy and Doll Museum*

ABOVE
Maker **Lehmann**
Marks *EPL* [in bell] *Marke Lehmann*
Date *1929–41*
Length **7½in (19cm)**
This post van was clearly a product of the 1930s as it displays the German eagle and swastika of the Nazi era. Similar items were produced without the swastika. Clockwork powered, the van has two opening rear doors and a roof rack. It is rare.

Left-hand motorcycle
Maker **Schuco (Schreyer & Co.)**
Marks *Schuco Motodrill*
Date **1960s**
Length **5in (13cm)**
This is the Schuco "Motodrill Clown", whose trick is to travel in a circle and then go into a sudden spin.

Right-hand motorcycle
Maker **Schuco (Schreyer & Co.)**
Marks *Made in the U.S. Zone, Germany*
      Schuco Curvo 1000
Date **1950s**
Length **5in (13cm)**
This ingenious toy – the Schuco "Curvo 1000" – can be programmed to travel in seven different patterns, from a circle to a complex star movement. The selection is made by turning the knob at the top of the steering column. Ingenious Schuco toys such as these are highly desirable, but they appear to have been produced in considerable quantity and are still fairly readily obtainable.

Schuco
PATENT
CURVO 1000

Der Tausendkünstler auf dem Motorrad

legt sich in kühner Schräglage in die Kurve und schwingt sich in der Geraden in die normale aufrechte Fahrstellung zurück. Durch Verstellen des Skalenzeigers mittels der Stellschraube führt Schuco-Curvo in verwegener Kurvenfahrt viele Figurenfahrten aus. Er wendet bei entsprechender Einstellung auch selbsttätig vor einem Hindernis und kann auch Karussellfahrten ausführen. Die herausziehbare Steckachse ermöglicht Vorderrad-Abnahme sowie Reifen-Montage.

Ein technisch interessantes, neues Schuco-Spielzeug, das jung und alt begeistert.

Ausstattung: Schwere Rennmaschine, aus starkem Blech, mehrfarbig bedruckt, Nickelverzierung. Abnehmbares Vorderrad mit Gummi-Hohlreifen, der auf die Felge montiert werden kann, Länge 12,5 cm, bunte Stückpackung, langlaufender Uhrwerkartikel.

Stellschraube zum Einstellen der jeweils gewünschten Fahrfigur
Steckachse zum Herausnehmen des Vorderrades — Werkaufzug
Abnehmbarer Gummireifen
Skala und Zeiger zum Ablesen der durch die Stellschraube eingestellten Fahrfigur — Stützfinger für Karusselfahrten — Arretier-Druckknopf für Werkstillstand und Einstellung zum Start

they have been a popular toy subject for almost as many years as tin toys have been manufactured. Tipp & Co. was responsible for a variety of especially interesting models – some with sidecars. Tipp – known either as Tipco or TCO – was founded in 1912, but its owner, Philip Ullmann, left Germany as a political refugee in 1933 and established the firm Mettoy in England.

Another German company, Arnold, which was founded in 1906 and

Left-hand motorcycle
Maker **Schuco (Schreyer & Co.)**
Marks *Schuco*
Date **1950s**
Length **4¾in (12cm)**

Right-hand motorcycle
Maker **Schuco (Schreyer & Co.)**
Marks *Schuco*
Date **1950s**
Length **4¾in (12cm)**
The left-hand motorcycle, "Carl 1005", travels round and round, heeling over realistically on the bends. The right-hand cycle, "Mirakamot 1012", is designed to run on a table. When it reaches the edge, a special mechanism turns it away before it can fall off. The sheer ingenuity of these and many others of the Schuco range of novelty toys makes them extremely desirable to collectors; therefore, although they may be found, they are usually fairly expensive.

Maker **Arnold**
Marks *A in a triangle*
Date **1930s**
Length **7½in (19cm)**
This motorcycle with a German soldier in the saddle dates from the 1930s and is a nicely lithographed toy. It bears the trademark that is earlier than, although not dissimilar to, that of Kellermann, for which it is sometimes mistaken. The toy is driven by clockwork, and this also illuminates the oversize headlamp by means of a flint and wheel mechanism, which was used also on "civilian" versions of this model. Because of a general interest in collecting model and toy motorcycles, these earlier examples are growing extremely hard to find.

initially made mostly boats and novelty toys, introduced the novelty motorcycle "Mac" in the 1950s: the rider pulls up and dismounts, pauses, remounts and drives away. This model was copied by the Japanese and reproduced in much larger scale as a battery toy, when the rider appeared also as a police motorcyclist. However, although motorcycles have always been a popular toy, very few tin, battery-operated examples were made. The most desirable are the German, wind-up versions.

Maker **Kellermann**
Marks *C.K.O.*
Date **1930s**
Length **5½in (14cm)**
This novelty motor cycle has a pillion passenger who leans over as the machine banks around corners and returns to the upright position when the cycle travels straight ahead. Powered by clockwork, it was made by Kellermann of Nuremberg. Examples turn up occasionally on toy-fair stalls and at auctions.

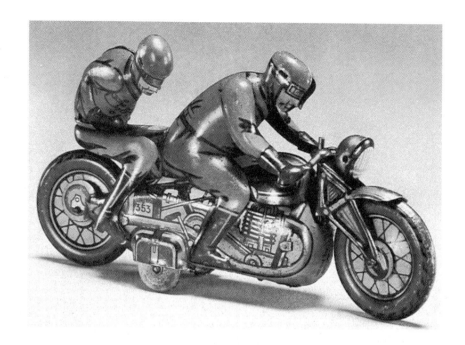

BUSES

Buses have been copied in tinplate for a great number of years, both single- and double-deckers. They often display interesting advertising announcing theatrical events or acting as a reminder of the commercial products of the time. One open-top double-decker bus even has a conductor who moves along the aisle on the top deck as the bus travels.

The American firm of Strauss was responsible for a clockwork double-decker "Inter-State Bus" in the 1920s, while many American-style modern "Greyhound" buses were produced for export by Japanese manufacturers in the 1960s and 1970s. Other Japanese-made toys were a sight-seeing bus – a passenger sticks his head out of a window as the bus rolls along – and a bus that sounds its horn as it moves forward.

Trams and trolleybuses were not forgotten by the toy manufacturers and many such vehicles originated in Germany. Trams often ran on their own tracks, and Bing and Märklin both made desirable electrically-powered versions.

The British trolleybus, now long gone, was remembered by such firms as Brimtoy and Betal. Brimtoy made many fine road vehicles (possibly in association with Bing), and the company's best products rivalled its German equivalents. It later amalgamated with Wells. Betal was the trademark used by the 1950s London toy wholesalers J. H. Glasman, Ltd.

And when the last Paris trolleybus was taken off the roads we were left a nice clockwork tinplate reminder of the vehicles that were once part of the busy Paris scene in the models made by Joustra.

Maker **Bing**
Marks *G.B.N.* in a diamond
Date c.1910
Length 11½in (29cm)
This clockwork bus is decorated with interesting lithographed advertisements redolent of the early years of the century in Britain. The model, too, contains much detail, including rubber tyres, a hand brake and a steering wheel that actually works. The passengers seated in this rare toy are by Märklin.

BOATS

Toy collectors refrain from differentiating between boats and ships – they tend to lump them altogether and call them toy boats, probably to the horror of all true sailors. However, it has to be admitted that the range of toy boats includes some of the most visually impressive toys ever made. The magnificent ocean-going liners and hefty battleships of the early 1900s often exceeded a metre in length. They were fitted out with all the intricate trappings and ornamentation of the time, sometimes even sporting a beautifully gilded replica of a traditional figurehead at the prow. These mighty models often carried the name of some popular real-life counterpart, even though there would probably be little actual resemblance. Many manufacturers gave their boats different names for different markets; for example one of Märklin's battleship models was

Maker **Unknown English**
Marks *Huntley & Palmers*
Date **1920s**
Length **17in (43cm)**

Maker **Unknown English**
Marks *Crawfords*
Date **1920s**
Length **18in (46cm)**
The biscuit tin in the shape of a steam launch was made to advertise the products of Huntley & Palmers, while "The Meteor", a

novelty biscuit tin, was made for Crawfords. The single headlamp on the radiator of "The Meteor" can be illuminated from a slim battery fixed under the chassis. These types of novelty containers were manufactured for the biscuit makers by several small firms, many of which were eventually absorbed into the Metal Box Co. The majority of them – especially those representing road, sea and air vehicles – are becoming quite rare and realizing high prices in auction sales. *Sotheby's*

OPPOSITE ABOVE
Maker **Betal**
Marks *Betal*
Date *c.*1950
Length (left-hand) 6¾in (17cm); (right-hand) 10½in (27cm)
Betal also sold these trolleybuses (without the trolleys) as motor buses. The buses illustrated here are probably rarer than the rather similar trolleybuses produced by Wells, and the larger of the two, while rare as a motor bus, is rarer still as a trolleybus. It is interesting to note the mis-spelling of "Leicester Square" on the destination boards of the larger bus – "ie" instead of "ei".

OPPOSITE BELOW
Left-hand bus
Maker **Wells**
Marks *Wells o' London* [between two wishing wells]
Date **1950s to 1960s**
Length **6¾in (17cm)**

Right-hand bus
Maker **Wells**
Marks *Wells o' London* [between two wishing wells]
Date **1950s and 1960s**
Length **8in (21cm)**
These two English-style trolleybuses were made by Wells. Both are in the red livery of London Transport and both have "piano wire" springs in their clockwork mechanisms. Both show different destination numbers although the licence plates are the same! Buses like this are not too difficult to find, but model transport enthusiasts – of which there are many – are always on the look out for examples.

Maker   **Märklin**
Marks   *G.M. & Cie.* [intertwined] in a shield
Date   *c.*1909
Length   **28¼in (72cm)**
This wonderfully detailed toy was based on
the transatlantic liner of the day, the
Carmania, which was owned by the White
Star Line. It was offered in two larger sizes in
Märklin's 1909 catalogue, all three toys being
powered by clockwork. A very rare item.

named *Weissenberg* in Germany, *H.M.S. Terrible* in Britain, and
New York in the United States.

These were, without doubt, toys for the children of wealthy families,
although many such smaller models were available. Clockwork was the
usual method of providing the power for the propeller – some models
needed twin propellers – although several were fitted with steam engines.
Steam pouring from the funnel obviously gave the toy the final touch of
realism.

Some of the smaller liners were powered by a geared flywheel motor.
Electric motors never seemed to become popular, and electrically
powered examples are rare. In the 1930s the English firm of Sutcliffe
introduced a 23in (60cm) motor-boat which had a 2-speed electric
motor, but the company soon reverted to clockwork mechanisms in its
subsequent models. Sutcliffe, which had started production in 1920 by

making simple battleships, originally favoured a type of water-circulatory motor heated by a spirit burner. This was basically a piece of U-shaped metal tubing with the two open ends protruding from the stern of the ship. The curved section was formed into a spiral under which the burner was placed. Because of the sound it makes in operation this device is often referred to as a "pop-pop" or "toc-toc" engine. Cheaper versions made in Germany and Japan appeared in penny toy boats, and these had similar motors heated from a piece of birthday-cake candle.

Toy boats were never as easy to make as other toys because they had to be waterproof and well painted. All joints had to be hand soldered and the hull hand painted to provide the best possible protection, operations that must have added to the cost of production.

Most of the very best toy boats were made in Germany. Märklin's range showed the same attention to detail and finishing as the company's other

Maker **Märklin**
Marks **G.M. & Cie. [intertwined] in a shield**
Date **c.1909**
Length **38½in (98cm)**
Here is Märklin's version of the sister ship of the *Carmania*, the *Mauretania*, at the time the largest ship in the world. (The third member of the family was the ill-fated *Lusitania*, which was torpedoed by the German navy in 1915.) The model was available with a clockwork, electric or steam-powered motor. It is very rare.

Maker **Carette**

Marks **None**

Date **1920s**

Length **17¾in (45cm)**

This photograph illustrates a nicely restored Carette liner. Old toys that have survived the years without a scratch are extremely hard to find. Many suffer minor damage and are best preserved in the condition in which they were found, with the original paintwork retained. Repainting should not be attempted unless absolutely essential, and the restoration of missing parts and repainting should, in any case, be left to experts with the skills necessary to re-create the missing pieces and achieve the authentic colours. The liner here has a clockwork motor. Interest in collecting model boats has escalated in the last few years, and all models are commanding high prices, especially the products of the better-known German manufacturers such as Carette, which produced some highly desirable models.

products – boats came complete with hand-painted flags, radio antennae and a wealth of detail that make these ships today extremely desirable and extremely expensive. Carette, a company founded in Nuremberg in 1886 by Frenchman Georges Carette, also produced fine hand-enamelled boats, including some smaller examples less than 5in (13cm) long. Another Nuremberg company, Fleischmann, included in its range 11 different sizes of the liner *Bremen* and experimented in the 1920s with a water-circulating engine heated by a methylated spirit burner.

Some splendid model boats were issued from the factory of Radiguet in Paris. Although they are not made from tinplate, the hulls being constructed from zinc, they are worth mentioning, for, with their wooden decks and masts, their brass boilers and funnels (they were steam powered) gleaming, they are most aesthetically pleasing.

In the United States the majority of toy boats seemed to be of the carpet toy variety and were fitted with wheels. Many of these models were not made from tinplate, but of wood covered with lithographed paper or of cast-iron. Carpet toy boats were also produced in Europe, but it seemed that the children on this side of the Atlantic preferred their toy boats to be water-borne.

In Britain the last of the tinplate toy manufacturers was the firm of Sutcliffe Pressings Ltd., which was based near Leeds, in the north of England. The firm was originally founded c.1895 by J. W. Sutcliffe, but it was not until 1920 that it began to manufacture toy boats. None of this firm's products could be compared with the magnificent models originating from France and Germany, but they were produced with an eye to economy for the less expensive side of the market and were well received for many years.

Maker **Fleischmann**
Marks **None**
Date **Late 1930s**
Length **19¾in (50cm)**
This handsome Fleischmann liner has a clockwork motor. Such items have appreciated greatly in value over the last few years, even sub-standard toy ships soon finding a buyer eager to restore them. Missing funnels, masts, rudders and even lifeboats can easily be authentically copied and replaced. *Sotheby's*

OPPOSITE ABOVE
Maker **Sutcliffe**
Marks *Sutcliffe*
Date **1978–80**
Length 12½in (32cm)

The *Valiant* battleship was produced by Sutcliffe in 1978 and was made in limited quantities until 1980. The toy boat, painted battleship grey and powered by clockwork, was specially designed to commemorate the firm's first boat, which appeared in 1928. Small differences in design were deliberately introduced to avoid any confusion with the original: for example, the aperture for the winding key was placed between the two funnels (in the original the winding stem was situated in one of the funnels). Produced as a limited edition, examples grow more difficult to find as interest in Sutcliffe items gradually increases.

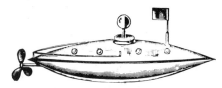

Three sizes of this clockwork submarine boat were offered for sale in Gamage's 1902 catalogue. The size shown here cost 10½d (approximately 4p), and the two larger sizes cost 1s 4½d (7p) and 2s 6d (12½p).

Right up to the closure of the factory in the early 1980s, Sutcliffe insisted on a high standard of workmanship for the fairly simple, but excellently produced, tinplate toys. The firm's closure triggered off an interest in its products, and Sutcliffe boats now figure in a number of international collections. However, they are still to be found on offer at swap meets at reasonable prices, and there may even be toyshops that still have examples in their storerooms. Sutcliffe boats are excellent pieces for new collectors who are unable to afford the high prices demanded for much older toys.

Early models represented battleships, and they were powered by a refined version of the "toc-toc" type of motor, which operated far more smoothly than the kind found in the cheaper, smaller toy boats imported from abroad. This engine, heated by a spirit-burner, consisted of coiled copper tubing of exact proportions to give the best possible performance from such a simple device. The heat caused this water-circulatory system to propel the model along realistically. Models were also powered by clockwork motors, which were imported from Germany until a faulty batch was delivered in the 1930s. This caused serious production problems, and the firm decided to manufacture its own mechanisms thereafter. Sutcliffe's first toy boats were 12in (30cm) and 16in (41cm) battleships. About 1928 a motor-cruiser with a copper "roof" was introduced, based on the 16in (41cm) hull. Only a very few were made, and no example is known to have survived. In 1930 the firm designed its largest model boat, a 24in (61cm) motor boat, which was in production for approximately three years. It was fitted with an electric motor powered by battery and offered a choice of two speeds. Few examples survive today. In the 1930s a number of speedboats, such as the *Minx* and *Meteor*, and the cruisers *Commodore*, *Swallow* and *Empress* were marketed. One of the more intricate Sutcliffe toys was the neat destroyer *Grenville* which was manufactured from 1938 to 1940.

The fashion for toy boats seemed to fade away after World War II, the ranges of ocean liners produced by the German firms of Arnold and Fleischmann being among the last. Sutcliffe closed in the early 1980s, after making a range of collectors' models of some of the firm's best known lines. Even the Japanese showed little interest in boats among the amazing range of tinplate toys being produced. They did make a few battery-operated carpet boats, including a tug-boat, a paddle-boat, an ocean liner and an aircraft carrier, and a rare Japanese water-borne toy was a submarine, powered by either battery or a flywheel mechanism.

Submarines have always proved to be fascinating toys, particularly if they could submerge and resurface realistically. Märklin introduced a fine clockwork model in which the mechanism controlled the hydrofoils. Bing produced various model submarines, and, in the 1930s, an Arnold submarine appeared as a U-Boat complete with Nazi markings. After the war it reappeared, without swastikas, and marked "Made in U.S. Zone".

In the 1930s Sutcliffe designed an attractive little clockwork submarine, the *Unda Wunda*, which was well made and proved a popular

LEFT
Kenneth Sutcliffe (*left*), son of the founder of Sutcliffe Pressings, Leeds, is seen discussing two of the firm's products with collector Mike Butler of Sheffield. Sutcliffe boats were mainly powered by clockwork, although the earlier models were driven by a simple form of steam engine.

The boat held by Mr Sutcliffe is the largest model the firm ever manufactured, and unusually it has an electric motor. The smaller boat, a 12in (30cm) cruiser, is named *Diana*, after the present Princess of Wales. This model was not supplied through the normal retail trade but was issued, complete with a specially designed box, especially to meet the demands of collectors. The Sutcliffe factory closed in 1982. There is increasing interest in Sutcliffe boats, but it is not too late to start collecting!

This beautifully enamelled ocean liner with six life boats and six guns is 26in (66cm) long. Sold for 70s (£3.50) in 1902, it was available in Britain as the *Oceanic* and in Germany as the *Kaiser Wilhelm*. It was propelled by steam.

toy. It appeared in different disguises throughout the years, the most famous of all being its appearance in the guise of the *Nautilus*, star of the Walt Disney movie *20,000 Leagues Under the Sea* in the mid-1950s.

The 1930s was a time of speed record attempts – everyone seemed to be setting out to break records in travel on land, sea and air – and toy manufacturers were quick to realize sales potential. Soon children were able to buy, or be given, toy racing boats galore made by such firms as Sutcliffe, Hornby and J.E.P. These were generally simple, well-made toys, with un-governed clockwork motors that allowed a quick burst of speed in imitation of the real thing. They covered only a short distance. Slower model motor-cruisers were available, which travelled greater distances but at slower speeds. The Hornby range of clockwork boats was produced up to World War II, never to reappear, although the models made by J.E.P. and Sutcliffe continued into the post-war years.

A steam torpedo boat – "fitted with powerful engine [and] beautifully japanned" – cost 17s 6d (87½p) in 1902.

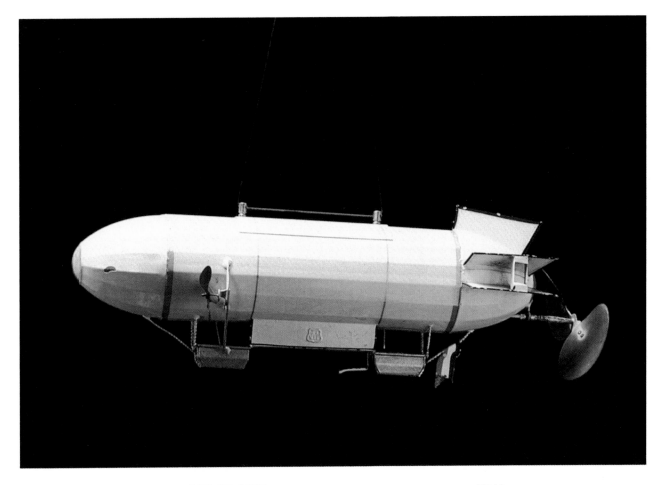

AIRCRAFT

Tinplate aircraft appeared in all shapes and forms over the years, often in imitation of their real-life counterparts but with varying degrees of accuracy. The first toy aircraft naturally reflected the curious inventions that first gave mankind the power of flight. Tinplate balloons and dirigibles, like the "heavier-than-air" machines that followed, became popular toys. The tinplate models were naturally too heavy to fly of their own accord and the illusion of flight was achieved by suspension from a piece of string. Some models were clockwork powered and fitted with oversize propellers, which could actually assist the dangling toy to achieve captured flight and travel, quite realistically, in a circle.

Captured flight of this sort was all the tinplate flying machine could ever really manage throughout its many decades of existence. Toys that could actually enjoy free flight needed to be made from lighter materials, such as balsa wood and silk. Clockwork motors were too heavy, and the only solution to the power problem for a long time was the simple elastic-band motor.

Maker **Märklin**
Marks *G.M. & Cie.* [intertwined] in a shield
Date **c.1909**
Length **9in (23cm)**
The airship was a means of flight that found much favour with toy makers, and Märklin reflected the contemporary interest in Count Zeppelin's gigantic constructions by issuing this toy. It could be "flown" suspended from above, with the clockwork motor operating the propeller. A rare toy.

RIGHT

Maker **Unknown Japanese**

Marks *Made in Japan*

Date **1930s**

Length **13in (33cm)**

This model of the ill-fated British airship the R-101 was made in Japan. When the airship is suspended by a thread of yarn, its clockwork motor spins the propeller sufficiently to allow the model to circle around in apparent flight. There is a fascination in toys commemorating the days of the early aeronauts, and examples are still to be found – at a price. *Sotheby's*

BELOW RIGHT

Maker **Oro-Werke (Neil, Blechschmidt & Müller)**

Marks *Orobr*

Date *c.*1914

Length **6¾in (17cm)**

Toys like this early clockwork-powered monoplane are hard to come by today. Airplanes are relative latecomers to the collecting scene. One of the drawbacks to such a specialist collection is the problem of display, especially of the larger models, which are difficult to accommodate in a normal showcase. Suspending them by a thread is one solution, but this has the disadvantage of displaying the underside, which is often neither realistic nor desirable. Another possibility is to display them vertically on walls. *Sotheby's*

OPPOSITE

Maker **Märklin**

Marks *G.M. & Cie.* [intertwined] in a shield

Date *c.*1909

Dimensions **17¼×15¾×8in (44×40×21cm)**

This is a fine example of an early flying machine of the type made famous by the pioneering activities of the Wright brothers. This marvellous toy is designed to allow the clockwork motor to propel it along the ground or to drive it along a suspended wire by means of a geared overhead pulley. The motor also powers the propeller. This toy is extremely rare.

Maker **Lehmann**
Marks *Lehmann*
Date **Early 1900s**
Length **6in (15cm)**
This curiosity from the German firm Lehmann is the "Ikarus", a primitive clockwork-powered flying machine toy. A rare toy, evocative of the pioneering days of flight. Sotheby's

A toy flying machine and its tinplate hangar – or, as the catalogue describes it, "flyerstation with flyer" – made by Distler, Germany, c.1920.

The first toys to appear followed the wave of public interest in the activities of the pioneer aeronauts at the beginning of this century. Their curious machines, especially the famous biplane of the Wright Brothers, were copied in toy form by some of the German companies, and existing examples of the fine models of the Wrights' plane produced by Märklin are extremely rare.

Besides being made to dangle on string, toy aircraft often appeared on carousel toys, their propellers (usually made from celluloid) whirling like children's toy windmills in the current of air created as they travelled round and round. Other planes were caused to rotate around tinplate towers of varying kinds, often in groups. One toy, made by Distler, featured a plane circling on the end of a wire over a hangar.

Many tinplate toy aircraft appeared in the years between the two world wars, including seaplanes and flying-boats, which would generally float on water, being moved forward by the pull of their own propellers. One

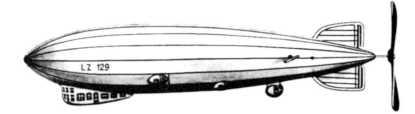

Tipp & Co's 1936 catalogue illustrated a selection of airships. This clockwork-powered example was fitted with electric lighting. Like the other airships made by Tipp, "LZ 129" could be "flown" suspended from a string, the large rear propeller causing it to circle around. The model illustrated is 14¾in (37cm) long.

ABOVE

Top left

Maker **Mettoy**

Marks *None*

Date **1950s**

Length **15in (38cm)**

This Mettoy jet airliner from the 1950s has two sparking engines and is powered by clockwork. It is a toy that was also produced in other liveries and with other propellers in the late 1930s. It vaguely represents the Douglas DC3 Dakota in outline, and although once a fairly common toy, it is growing more difficult to buy.

Top right

Maker **Unknown**

Marks *Paris-Tokyo* printed on the sides

Date **1930s**

Length **13¾in (35cm)**

The French-made biplane has a clockwork motor. Quite a few tinplate airplanes originated in France, including some interesting examples from the company Joustra. This biplane would be hard to acquire.

Below

Maker **Tipp**

Marks *TCO* monogram

Date **1950s**

Length **23¾in (60cm)**

The large Tipp turbo-prop airliner in the livery of Lufthansa is powered by batteries from the separate, hand-held controls. This is an interesting example of a battery toy that was *not* made in Japan. Schuco also made battery-operated airplanes, but it was the Japanese toy makers of the 1960s who developed the full potential of electrically-powered toys. *Sotheby's*

One of Gebrüder Einfalt's 1930s toys: the gradual movement downwards of the two aircraft caused them to spiral around the stand, their propellers spinning in the air current. Einfalt produced a similar toy in which small aircraft "flew" around a lighthouse.

Above

Maker **Lehmann**

Marks *EPL–II 652 Marke Lehmann* [bell] *Made in Germany* printed on sides

Date 1920–30

Length **9¾in (25cm)**

Below

Maker **Lehmann**

Marks *Made in Germany* [bell] *Marke* printed on side

Date 1920–30

Length **5½in (14cm)**

Both these Lehmann toys – the EPL II Zeppelin and one of the firm's many novelty road vehicles, the delivery van known as "Aha" – distinctively display the firm's trademark. All Lehmann toys are collectable, and these two examples are especially so. The company produced many toys, and examples are usually available although expensive. Mint and boxed items are, obviously, even more expensive. *Sotheby's* fine example, made in the late 1930s by Fleischmann, was a representation of the fabulous 12-engined giant Dornier flying-boat. The engines were not powered, but the toy was given an extra propeller to pull the craft along the surface of the water.

Most toy aircraft were designed to be pushed or driven along the floor by clockwork, although the mechanics often included revolving propellers. Later, battery-powered models permitted a little more sophistication – realistic winking lights, lighted interiors and engine sounds. Frequently, like the *Vickers Viscount* airliner produced in different liveries by Schuco in the 1950s, they incorporated phased engine action. Here the engines start up in sequence, simulating the ritual engine-testing carried out before take-off, followed by the plane taxi-ing forward. Similar and even more complex actions were built into Japanese battery-toy models of the same period. One model even has the passengers moving away from the windows and an air hostess opening the exit door after the plane has drawn to a halt. But the actual take-off and flight of any of these heavier tinplate models was an insoluble problem for all of the world's toy makers.

Maker **Girard Model Works Inc.**
Marks *Marx U.S.A.*
Date 1920s–1930s
Length 12½in (32cm)
This American-made tinplate toy monoplane was marketed by Louis Marx of New York and made by the Girard Model Works Inc. of Pennsylvania. The clockwork mechanism propels the plane forwards and causes the propeller to revolve "at great speed". This is a fairly hard toy to find.
Sotheby's

Toy aircraft were produced in most toy-making countries – Germany, the United States, Spain, France and Britain. Märklin in Germany and Meccano in England introduced popular aeroplane construction outfits during the 1930s, and another German firm, Markes & Co., under its tradename Dux, made interesting construction outfits, one of the commonest being the notorious Stuka dive-bomber. Earlier, Dux had issued a set for the construction of a model of the great Dornier DoX 12-engined flying-boat.

Tipp & Co. marketed an interesting tinplate high-wing lightweight bomber, which had a clockwork mechanism designed to release bombs hanging from beneath the wings. They fell in sequence and, being fitted with toy-pistol caps, actually exploded on impact. These toy planes were issued with different markings, some of them incorporating swastikas in the livery.

Helicopters, developed from the autogyro of the 1930s, have been the subject of many toys, and a variety of models hailed from Japanese manufacturers from the 1950s to the 1970s. Many could imitate flight – with the aid of a piece of string – but the German firm of Arnold made a toy that actually did operate realistically. It was attached to a bowden cable and the operator powered it by winding a handle at the opposite end. It was captured flight but, with a little care, quite authentic manoeuvres could be performed – including perfect take-off and landing.

NOVELTY TOYS

All tinplate toys are, by their very nature, novelties, but many were specifically designed to amuse. Novelty toys are particularly pleasant, and their amusing, often crazy, antics bring a smile to the face. They have great appeal for children of all ages because their clever creators knew that they must also attract the attention of the parents who had the spending power! A toy ship, car or railway engine is expected to be enjoyed fairly seriously by the imaginative child, even if it is far from being an accurate miniature representation of the original. The novelty toy ship, railway engine or whatever, provides lighthearted amusement for both young and old alike.

Time has added to the attraction of such toys and their appeal has increased over the years. Many are playthings that would not be commercially viable to the more sophisticated children of today, but they were produced in millions through the ages, many of them being designed with modified actions of the superior "princely toys", the automata of the wealthy.

A novelty whale fitted with, according to Gamage's 1902 catalogue, "a strong clockwork movement"!

Maker   **Unknown**
Marks   *Made in Germany*
Date   **1920s**
Length   **5in (13cm)**

Here is a toy with an amusing action: it makes a rocking, swivelling, jerking journey, travelling spasmodically backwards and forwards until the spring of the clockwork motor exhausts itself. A very similar German-made toy is shown in the Moko catalogue for 1926. Several American toys have been designed with similar actions, and they are known as "whoopee toys". A fairly rare item.

Maker   **Philip Vielmetter**
Marks   *Ph.V.F. Artist* [in a pentagon]
         Schutz Marke
Date   **Early 1900s**
Height   **5½in (14cm)**

A series of cams allows "The Artist" to be programmed to draw sketches of a number of contemporary and 19th-century personalities – Queen Victoria, the Czar of Russia, Disraeli and so forth – on paper placed on the easel. Operated by winding the handle at the rear of the figure, this toy was made in Germany in the early 1900s by Philip Vielmetter, a toy maker who apparently produced just this one piece. Rare examples of similar toys made in England and France are known to exist. This is an expensive toy, but examples occasionally appear in auction sales, sometimes with the original box and a good selection of the necessary cams. Sometimes a sheet illustrating the various figures to be drawn is included. *Sotheby's*

Dog and cat

Maker **Schuco (Schreyer & Co.)**

Marks *Schuco*

Date **1930s**

Length **4¾in (12cm)**

The dog and the cat are clockwork, felt-covered tinplate figures, made by Schuco during the 1930s. They were the forerunner of the similar "Scottie" dog, which continued to be produced after World War II. Each animal's rear is supported on two metal "feet", which are linked to two almost hidden wheels; the feet balance the toy as it travels forwards. Linked to the wheels are the two front legs, which, although purely for visual effect, alternate realistically as the animal moves. These two items are relatively hard to find, although post-war examples of the company's Scotch Terrier "Nipper" are easier to come across.

Boy and bear

Maker **Unknown Japanese**

Marks **None**

Date **1950s or 1960s**

Height **7in (18cm)**

The boy and the bear are two versions of the same toy. The book each holds has metal pages, which are flicked over by means of a magnet in the toy's right hand (or paw). Each time a page is turned, the toy's head jerks. These toys are relatively hard to find, although items occasionally appear at sales. Given the current interest in Teddy Bears, the bear model could now be in even greater demand.

OPPOSITE

A selection of Schuco (Schreyer & Co.) novelty figures from a 1930s catalogue. These are *Tanzfiguren* (dancing figures), but others drummed, played violins and moved around. The figures were clad in fabric and were between 4½ and 5½in (11–14cm) tall.

One instance of such a toy is the tinplate "Artist", which appears to be the only toy made by the German firm of Vielmetter in the 19th century. In this toy we have a very simplified version of the famous "Writer" or "Draughtsman", two of the intricately constructed automata of the 18th-century genius Jaquet-Droz, which are preserved in the Neuchatel Art & History Museum, Switzerland. While "The Artist" is a far inferior android in every respect, it is fair to consider it a superior toy. Its mechanism may be a great deal simpler but it depends upon similar principles in its operation. Hand wound (there is no clockwork motor), the figure – a clown – will execute an acceptable sketch on a piece of paper fixed to his easel. It is programmed by the insertion of special cams in the base of the toy and these control the arm movements necessary to draw the figure. A number of these cams were supplied with the toy to produce likenesses of contemporary personalities such as Queen Victoria, the Czar of Russia and Louis XIV.

Not all novelty toys depended on intricate mechanisms, and many had nothing more than a simple clockwork motor to provide repetitive action. The German company Schreyer & Co. under its tradename Schuco issued a host of fascinating figures that did little more than frantically "wobble", the mechanism being fitted with a weighted governor to produce a peripatetic movement. Secondary action was given to some of these amusing figures to turn them into violinists or jugglers, and even, during the Nazi regime, cause them to raise one arm up and down in a salute.

Lehmann was famous for its range of amusing toys, including "Ski-Rolf", a skier who trundles along on his skis; "Tut Tut", the erratically driven car with a trumpet-blowing driver; "Tom", the climbing monkey;

Schuco-Tanzfiguren

mit mechanischen Bewegungen, Blechgehäuse mit buntem Stoffüberzug, Uhrwerkartikel.

Figuren und Tiere, die während des Tanzes abwechselnd irgendeinen Gegenstand z. B. Baby, Leiter etc. in die Höhe heben und wieder absetzen.

Nr. 955 Tanz-Maus
mit Baby, Höhe 11 cm

Nr. 956 Tanz-Hase mit Baby
Höhe 11,5 cm

Nr. 958 Tanz-Zwerg mit Zwerglein,
entweder mit Spitzhut oder Pilzhut,
Höhe 14 cm

In der gleichen Ausführung wie Nr. 955 wird auch angefertigt: **Nr. 960 Tanz-Maus** mit Baby, schwarz-weiß gekleidet, Höhe 11 cm. **Nr. 957 Tanz-Bär** mit Baby, Höhe 11 cm.

Nr. 932 Tirolerin mit Wickelkissen
und herausnehmbarem Baby.
Höhe 13 cm.

Nr. 933 Holländerin mit
Wickelkissen und herausnehmbarem
Baby. Höhe 13 cm

Nr. 934 Spreewälderin mit
Wickelkissen und herausnehmbarem Baby. Höhe 13 cm

In gleicher Ausführung und Größe wird auch angefertigt:
Nr. 930 Schwarzwälderin mit Wickelkissen und Baby, **Nr. 931 Breisgauerin** mit Wickelkissen und Baby.

Nr. 997 7 Feuerwehrmann
mit Leiter, Höhe 13 cm

Nr. 941 Tanzzwerg mit
Laterne u. Hämmerchen,
Höhe 14 cm

Nr. 983 8 Tirolerin mit
Alpenstock, Höhe 14 cm

Nr. 989 Kapitän mit
Fernglas, Höhe 13 cm

In einer ähnlichen Ausführung wie die Nr. 997 7 wird auch angefertigt:
Maus als Schlotfeger mit Leiter Nr. 967 Seppl mit Leiter Nr. 982 7.

RIGHT AND FAR RIGHT

Maker **Schuco (Shreyer & Co.)**

Marks *Schuco*

Date 1930s

Height 4¾in (12cm) (on average)

Schuco manufactured a variety of novelty figures, most about 4¾in tall. A counterweighted governor on the clockwork mechanism provided each figure with a peripatetic movement, and the mechanism also generally provided other actions – the "juggling" of the clown the raising and lowering of the naval officer's binoculars, the "fiddling" movement of the violinist and the drumming and cymbal playing of the clown on the right. These figures were made both before and after World War II.

Schuco figures from the 1930s, such as those shown below, often included German soldiers. Basically tinplate, the figures are neatly clad in fabric clothing. These figures are extremely collectable all over the world, although some models are more commonly found than others. They form a charming collecting theme.

and "Gustav", the miller who climbs a windmill to bring down a sack of flour on his head.

The German toy industry was responsible for a vast range of novelties, and one need only glance through the catalogues of exporter Moses Kohnstam to appreciate the immense varieties that his firm alone handled. Illustrated are jousting knights, comical clowns, organ-grinders, acrobats, pecking hens, billiard players, carousels, loop-the-loop aeroplanes, switch-backs, figures on see-saws and so on. These products represented the output of many German toy makers, which often used Kohnstam's company Moko as a distributor.

Another German concern that had a large output of novelty toys was Gebrüder Einfalt, which was responsible for a fascinating range of track toys in the years immediately after World War II. These toys, always colourfully presented, had an appeal of their very own, with tiny clockwork vehicles whizzing along tinplate tracks past decorative lithographed scenery. Simple, but effective, control systems allowed the vehicles to interweave along the tracks, halting where necessary to avoid collision where the railway tracks or roads crossed. The vehicles sometimes disappeared into mountain tunnels, mysteriously reappearing at a different level to free-wheel downhill. Some of the lay-outs even incorporated moving miniature human figures, which were activated by hidden leverage from a passing vehicle.

About the same time the German firm of Arnold introduced its

Maker **Lehmann**
Marks *EPL* **cypher in a bell**
Date **1920s**
Length **7½in (19cm)**
One of Lehmann's rare novelty toys is "Ski Rolf", seen here with the original box. The skier's belt-buckle acts as a switch to start and stop the clockwork mechanism, which propels the toy forward in a realistic manner. "Ski Rolf" is quite difficult to find.

Maker **Lehmann**
Marks *Lehmann* and bell trademark on sole
of shoes
Date **1910**
Height **7½in (19cm)**
Lehmann's clockwork "Sailor" staggers
about drunkenly, and, as an added novelty,
he even dances standing on his head! The
cap-band bears the words *H.M.S.
Dreadnought.* The "Sailor" is not too difficult
to find.

wonderful motorcyclist "Mac". As the clockwork powered bike travelled along "Mac" would brake to a stop and realistically dismount, standing by the side of his machine. Then he would cock his leg back over the saddle, sit down and drive off!

In France Fernand Martin of Paris was responsible for a huge output of novelty toys. His company started production towards the end of the 19th century, and one of its most interesting products is the "Mysterious Ball", which is based on a popular contemporary circus act in which a ball travels up a spiral track to the top of a pole and then opens to reveal the figure of a man inside. Other Martin toys include a clockwork walking English policeman, a pianist who plays a simple French melody, a swimming fish and a mechanical gymnast.

American manufacturers produced many novelty toys in tinplate, and early examples include horse-drawn novelties such as the "Trotter" by Ives and the "Galloping Horse" by the Stevens & Brown Manufacturing Co. Many American toys were influenced by characters from the popular strip and movie cartoons of the day. Louis Marx commemorated "Li'l Abner", a celebrated star in the realms of American comic strip cartoons, with his famous "Dogpatch Band" piano toy. It was based on the earlier "Mouse Orchestra" toy in which four mouse-figures are assembled around a piano.

After World War II Japan emerged as the world's leading toy producer and German domination of the international market declined. An astonishing number of well-produced tinplate novelty toys from Japan flooded into the toyshops of the world, and many of them were powered by clockwork or friction motors. However, Japanese manufacturers also introduced an amazing range of battery-operated tinplate toys, which added a new dimension to novelty actions, and these are discussed on pages 86–93.

CHARACTER TOYS

A specialist area of toy collecting is dedicated to popular comic characters emulated in toy form. This is a peculiarly American interest, largely because of the many newspaper strip cartoons published in the 1920s and 1930s. The "funnies", as these popular colour-printed newspaper supplements were known, often also found their way over to Britain in the 1930s to be sold cheaply by street traders. Characters such as L'il Abner, Popeye the Sailorman, Mutt & Jeff, The Yellow Kid, the Katzenhammer Kids and a host of others captivated their American audiences. Popeye, of course, also appeared in many animated movie cartoons, but the most famous characters of all, were the products of the Disney studios, which could claim a world-wide following.

Cartoon characters were copied profusely by toy makers in the years both before and after World War II – even the crusty old Mr Magoo and the mischievous Tom and Jerry were included in the stream of battery toys that came from Japan.

A popular cartoon figure from the early days of "moving pictures" was

Felix the Cat, which became the subject of quite a few novelty toys, including one of Felix apparently operating a hand-powered three-wheeler cart – the real motivation of the toy came from a clockwork motor, of course – made by Ingap of Italy in the 1930s.

Mickey Mouse, often accompanied by Minnie, featured regularly in toy form from very soon after their first screen appearance in 1928, and they continued to do so when tin toys gave way to plastic. Donald Duck was another favourite, and Schuco made a popular toy of him in the days before cosmetic surgery shortened his bill. Schuco reintroduced Donald in the 1960s in an animated mixture of tinplate and plastic. Even the faithful Pluto appeared in toy form, in one instance riding one of the Lionel novelty trains and in another as an animated dancer accompanying Donald Duck in a clockwork toy by Marx named "Donald Duck's Duet".

Mickey and Minnie are reputed to have saved the American toy railway firm Lionel from certain bankruptcy in the 1930s when the mice featured in the Mickey Mouse handcar set, which was one in a series of boxed gauge O clockwork sets. Other handcars were made with Donald Duck and Pluto, Peter Rabbit and that most benevolent character of all, Father Christmas.

A similar toy to the Lionel handcar and also featuring Mickey Mouse and Minnie appeared on sale in the United Kingdom at about the same time. It was accompanied by another toy with the two mice from Walt Disney's *Cinderella*. Both were made by Wells Brimtoy, which also produced the Mickey Mouse Circus Train. The train had a moving figure of Mickey shovelling coal into the firebox of a miniature replica of a contemporary British steam locomotive, the *Silver Link*.

German manufacturers were quick to enter into the American character toy market, and a popular toy made by Distler in the 1930s featured Mickey Mouse as an "organ grinder" with a diminutive Minnie performing a jig on top of the instrument, which issued a few simple musical notes as Mickey turned the handle. H. Fischer & Co. of Nuremberg turned out an excellent model of the Fontaine Fox curiosity the Toonerville Trolley in the late 1920s. It had a specially designed eccentric mechanism to make the crazy vehicle proceed on its erratic journey.

Many figures inspired by cartoon characters were produced by the Swiss firm of A. Bucherer, which produced a series of articulated metal dolls with composition heads, hands and feet in the 1920s. Although some of these figures were based on real personalities, others featured comic characters, such as figures from the American strip cartoons, including the series "The Katzenjammer Kids" also known as "The Captain and the Kids".

Charlie Chaplin is one of the most familiar of the human characters to have been commemorated in toy form, and one of the best known examples was made by Schuco. This toy was presumably manufactured in the firm's early days because neither the figure nor the box carries any

Maker **Marx**
Marks *MAR* [over an] *X* within a circle.
      Made in England
Date **1930s**
Height **7½in (19cm)**

"Smokey Joe", the climbing fireman, is a tinplate clockwork figure, which climbs the ladder and knows that he has to stop when he gets to the top. This toy was made by the American firm Marx at its English factory at Dudley near Birmingham. The figure reappeared in the 1950s but made from plastic. The later version of this with the plastic figure is fairly common but is not as desirable as the rarer tinplate version.

Maker **Schreyer & Co.**
Marks **None; box is marked** *Foreign*
Date **1920s**
Height **6¼in (16cm)**

A clockwork Charlie Chaplin made by Schreyer & Co. evidently before it adopted the "Schuco" trademark. No name or trademark appears even on the original box, only the words "Made in Germany". The company was founded by the partners Schreyer and Müller in 1912, and Charlie Chaplin must have been one of its earliest productions, also appearing dressed as a chef and as a cowboy. It is not too difficult to find the famous "Little Tramp" figure, but the other variations are quite rare.

reference to the maker. Chaplin was featured wearing the outfit for which he was most famous and twirling his familiar cane. Other, rarer versions of this particular toy depict him as a chef and as a cowboy. Popular European characters, either real or fictional, rarely appeared in toy form, although in the 1930s Schuco made a small clockwork toy based on a strip cartoon from the *Berliner Illustrirten* called "Father and Son". It consisted of two separate figures, the balding moustachioed father (which contained the clockwork motor) and the young son. The figures could be made to join hands by means of an early form of adhesive plastic and could perform various simple acrobatics when set in motion.

Batman, complete with cape, appeared as an impressive walking battery toy made in Japan in the 1960s. He has also appeared in a tinplate

Maker **Unknown Japanese**
Marks **None**
Date **1950s**
Height **11in (28cm)**

The strong band of Disneyana collectors has helped to make this toy hard to find today. "Mickey the Magician" is an attractive piece with an amusing action based on a popular type of early automata in which a conjuror would seem to cause objects to disappear and reappear. Mickey does this with a tinplate chicken: he covers it with a top hat, waves his wand and squeaks a few indecipherable magic words. When he removes the hat, hey presto, the chicken has gone. Mickey replaces the hat, repeats his actions, and the chicken is once again revealed when the hat is raised.

This character toy by Schuco (Schreyer & Co.) is from the *Berliner Illustrierten* strip cartoon of the 1930s known as "Father and Son". The pictures show the action.

Schuco-Tanzfiguren.

Vater und Sohn als Akrobaten und Tänzer

Patentamtl. geschützt

Die lustigen Figuren der „Berliner Jllustrirten"

D. R. Patent   D. R. G. M.

Die inneren Handflächen des Vaters sind mit einer Wachsmasse versehen, an die der Sohn in unzähligen lustigen Stellungen befestigt werden kann. Das im Innern der Handfläche des Vaters befindliche Wachs wird durch Fingerwärme haftfähig.

Batmobile, a battery-operated model car, accompanied by the faithful Robin. Superman featured in an early 1950s battery toy that portrays him struggling to push backwards an advancing military tank. He is successful, of course, and lifts the tank into the air. Like the Batmobile, the Superman toy originated in Japan. These and other character toys such as Godzilla overlap into the realms of fantasy toys (see page 97), but their basic tinplate construction makes them a valid subject for collection.

BATTERY TOYS

After World War II Japan launched a tremendous attack on the toy markets of the world, and a range of colourful novelty tinplate toys pushed Germany out of the lead it had held for many decades. Japan had previously been known as a manufacturer of cheap, shoddy goods; now it was delivering an amazingly wide selection of well-made, well-designed and ingenious playthings.

Many of the first products were variations on earlier toys, but it soon became evident that Japan was taking a new approach to toy making by concentrating on the production of a range of battery-operated items. By

Maker **Tipp & Co.**
Marks *TCO* monogram
Date **1930s**
Length **12in (31cm)**

Here is a real fantasy toy from the 1930s: a nicely lithographed Father Christmas is at the steering wheel, and the body of the car is decorated with illustrations of the kind of toys he would be expected to carry in his sack during the festive season. Just to complete the atmosphere, the car carries an illuminated Christmas tree, which is powered from a battery concealed under the vehicle. This fantastic toy is very rare.

Maker **Masutoku Toy Factory**
Marks *M.T.* [in a diamond]
Date **1960s**
Height **7in (18cm)**

"Bear the Cashier" is the name of this jolly little Japanese battery toy. Seated at an office desk, the bear busily starts operating her adding machine until she is interrupted by the ringing of the telephone. She picks it up, answers it (with a few squeaks), replaces it and carries on with her work. This is just one of the very many ingenious battery-operated toys introduced by the Japanese in the post-World War II years. A popular toy that is not too scarce.

BLACK BUTTON
MAIN SWITCH
PRESS TO START
PRESS TO STOP

WHITE BUTTON
ERASE AND RECORD
PRESS TO ERASE AND RECORD
WHILE TOY IS RUNNING

TALK   TALK
TALK
YAKKITY   YAKKITY
TALK   TALK
TALK   TALK
TALK

Pete
the
PARROT

HE REPEATS
EVERYTHING
HE HEARS

by MARX

© LOUIS MARX & CO INC MCMLXII

means of small electric motors and ingenious linkages, models and figures were able to perform all kinds of movements that would tax the powers of a clockwork mechanism. Furthermore, some of the electricity could be diverted for illumination purposes – even to producing smoke.

An example of what a battery toy can do is given by the not uncommon type known as "Charlie Weaver" (based on an American vaudeville character created by Cliff Arquette) or "The Bartender". Both are variations of the same basic toy, and their actions portray the shaking of a cocktail and the motions of taking a drink, which causes the figure's face to turn red, smoke to pour out of his ears and his body to sway from side to side. The change of colour is brought about by small electric bulbs within the translucent vinyl face, and the smoke is led to the ears from a smoke generator wired up within the figure. This apparatus is an electric filament sealed into a container of light machine oil. When the heat is turned on the resulting smoke is channelled to wherever it is required to emerge. It is a device that was also used to produce smoke from toy locomotives and car radiators. Some of the character figures made in Japan were also, by this method, allowed to appear to be realistically smoking a cigar or pipe.

It was now possible to add lifelike sirens and other sounds to add interest to toys, and some models incorporated a small tape-reproducer taking its sound from an endless loop of tape. Thus the Monkees, for instance, in their model "Monkeemobile" car were able to sing out their famous signature tune "We are the Monkees". Another toy depending on a built-in tape machine is "Pete the Parrot", a full-sized battery operated model of a parrot with eyes that light up, a head that turns and a beak that moves as he talks. Yes, Pete certainly talks and will repeat any phrase you tell him, gently flapping his wings as he does so. In the base of his perch is a hidden tape-recorder, which records your voice as long as you keep a button pressed down. Press another button and you get playback, with "Pete" busily miming the words.

Battery toys can also blow bubbles, and various toys take advantage of this facility, which depends on a small wire loop being dipped into a container of liquid detergent and then placed in front of a current of air created by a small rotating fan so giving a stream of lovely bubbles. You could choose from a number of toys – the "Bubble Blowing Boy", a "Bubble Blowing Elephant" and a "Bubble Blowing Musician" (he has trouble with his trumpet) to name but three.

One ingenious toy, working from a special cam to control the movements, is of "Topo Gigio" (the Italian character mouse, once a T.V. star) seated at a xylophone. Switch on and he carefully picks out the tune "London Bridge is Falling Down". Not a recording this: the tune is actually played by "Topo". Similar toys feature "Pinocchio" or "Dennis the Menace" (the American version of Dennis is a different character from the British Dennis).

It is obvious that Japanese manufacturers were designing the majority of their toys to please the vast American market. Although many found

Maker	**Marx**
Marks	*"Pete the Parrot" by Marx, 1962* and *Made in Japan* printed on instruction booklet inside box
Date	**1960s**
Height	18½in (47cm)

One of the largest battery toys of all, "Pete the Parrot" will repeat anything you say to him, thanks to an in-built tape recorder in the base. When he answers back, his beak moves, his eyes light up and his wings flutter. Not an easy toy to find in Europe since the majority of Japanese novelty toys were aimed at the vast North American market.

Maker   **Unknown Japanese**
Marks   **None**
Date   **1950s–1960s**
Height   **10in (26cm) on average**

"Piggy Cook" was a popular battery toy during the 1950s and 1960s. The figure, topped by its chef's hat, busies itself over a glowing stove, tossing and seasoning an omelette in a frying pan. The action repeats itself over and over again as long as the power is switched on. There are other, similar models, such as "Doggy Chef", "Bear Chef" and "Cuty Cook", the latter having the stylized head of either a hippopotamus or an elephant. All have the swaying, frying-pan-flipping action, but "Doggy Chef" can also move his eyes and ears, while "Bear Chef" and "Cuty Cook" can move their heads. "Piggy Cook" and "Doggy Chef" should be cooking tinplate omelettes, but the other figures cook hamburgers. "Piggy Cook" is more commonly found than the other figures in this range.

their way to Europe, some are rarely seen on this side of the Atlantic, unless they are brought over by a collector. Among these rarely seen toys are the fabulous "Haunted House" and the "Whistling Tree". The "Haunted House" is a largely tinplate (with a little plastic) model of a weird looking cottage. When buttons at the side are pressed, all kinds of strange things happen: a blind at a window moves; a black cat jumps up; the door opens to reveal a vampire; a ghost flits past a lighted window; and a skeleton appears out of the chimney, all to the accompaniment of hair-raising ghostly sounds. The "Whistling Tree" is a tree stump with a face and branch arms. It trundles along, its eyes and mouth opening and closing and its arms swinging as it goes whistling by!

There are battery-operated clowns galore doing everything from acrobatics to playing musical instruments. One of these, "High Jinx at the Circus", taxes its power output to the utmost. His head moves, he blows a whistle, his nose lights up, he balances a cymbal-playing monkey at the end of an extending ladder and he beats time with his foot. Some toy! "Pinky the Clown", on the other hand, merely blows a whistle while he juggles one ball from hand to hand and balances another ball on a rod extending from his nose, and the "Cyclist Clown" just pedals his tricycle backwards and forwards, his head moving up and down and his eyes moving from side to side while a bell rings and the headlamp on the tricycle lights up.

As we have already seen (page 50), many battery toys were produced in the form of model cars, but other road vehicles such as agricultural tractors, lorries and even tanks were also made. While some were

Maker **Unknown Japanese**
Marks *Marx* [in a circle over] *X*
Date 1950s
Height 15in (38cm)

If there were an award for the most curious toy ever made, the Japanese battery toy known as "The Whistling Tree" would certainly be a strong contender. Cleverly combining fantasy with ingenuity, the manufacturers introduced this strange plaything for the North American market. It is known to exist in at least two different, although similar, lithographed finishes, and it carries the Marx trademark. This weird toy will shuffle along on its "push and go" mechanism, whistling as it moves; its mouth opens and closes and its eyes blink. An additional feature is the crown of leaves, which lifts up and down as the tree shuffles forward! A strange and rare toy.

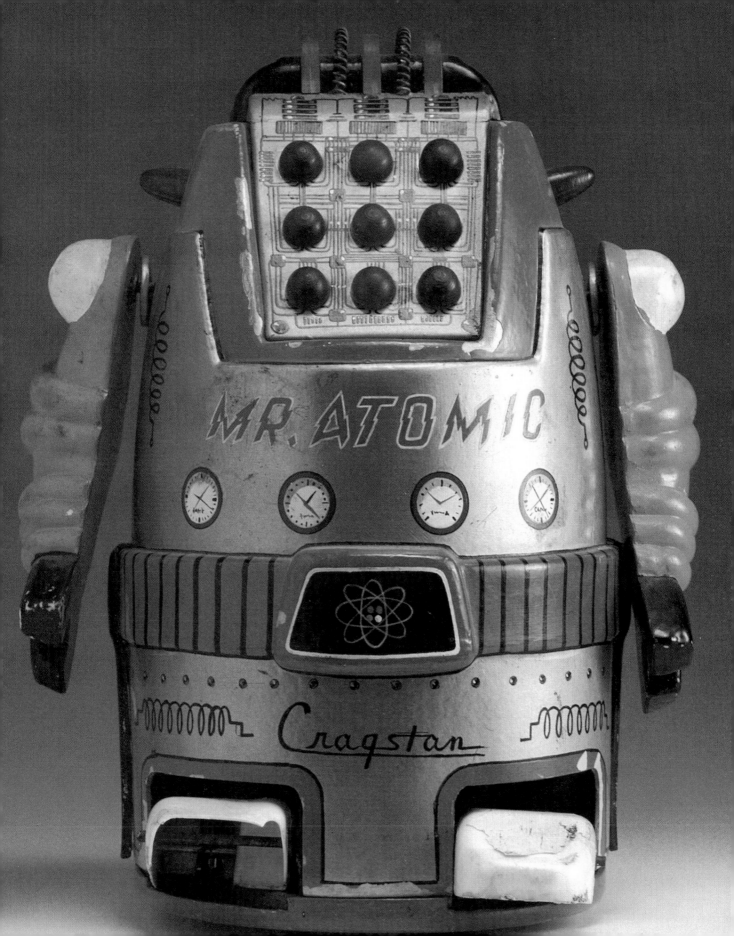

Maker **Unknown Japanese**
Marks **None**
Date **1950–60**
Height **10in (26cm)**
Inexperienced collectors often refer to figures such as this as robots. More experienced collectors know differently – this is an astronaut because there's supposed to be a human in there somewhere. A Japanese battery toy, this example is rarely found in this particular colour. One of the antennae from the top of his head is missing. A surge of interest in toy robots over the last few years has led to a scarcity of these space-fantasy items.
Courtesy Chester Toy and Doll Museum

Occasionally tinplate robots may be discovered that did not originate in Japan. However, these are exceptional. Earlier models contained none or very little plastic, but as the years passed more and more plastic was introduced into the designs, often to ornamental advantage. This was the case with all toys produced from the 1950s onwards, until plastic took the place of all but the most indispensable metal components.

Space toys, including rocket-ships, flying saucers and strange planetary vehicles are also desirable – as long as they are fantasy creations – and the more bizarre they are, the better. The more closely they resemble something out of an old Buck Rogers movie, the better they appear to be appreciated, and there is far less interest in toys modelled after real-life space vehicles.

All these toys are a mixture of mechanics and art. The robot is a personal creation of its designer, working within the constraints imposed upon him by the commercial demands of the production of the toy. The artist is copying nothing in most cases, unless he has been engaged to model a toy on another popular fantasy creature such as, say, the creature "Godzilla".

"Godzilla" is a toy that ambles along, roaring, and exhaling smoke, like the original monster creature created by Japanese moviemakers. "King Kong" has appeared in toy form, too, in both clockwork and battery-operated versions. He roars and beats his chest, just like the Hollywood version.

Such fantasy characters as "Batman" and "Superman" have found themselves miniaturized in tinplate form by Japanese toy makers and brought to a limited form of life through battery power, but here we are beginning to depart from the realm of fantasy toys and to move into the very similar world of novelty toys.

CATALOGUES AND EPHEMERA

Catalogue collecting is a rewarding side interest for the toy enthusiast. Prices vary according to age and the demand for the toys of a particular manufacturer; mint examples are well worth having, although they naturally command higher prices. Some of the early catalogues, such as the ones issued by Bing before World War I, were bound in hard covers. Damaged editions of these need the attention of a professional bookbinder in their restoration.

Paperback editions, such as the famous series Hornby Book of Trains from the late 1920s and 1930s, were prone to damage. Loose covers and pages need careful attention – some heavy-handed people would be well advised to leave this work to someone with the ability to carry out a neat repair. On no account should normal office adhesive tape be used; a special transparent matt tape is available from stationers which is almost invisible. Publicity leaflets, instruction leaflets, instruction booklets (such as the ones included with Meccano outfits), small posters and showcards my all have small tears mended this way. The tap is also useful for repairing toy cartons.

Maker **Unknown Japanese**
Marks **Marx Toys – Copyright Louis Marx & Co. Inc. Made in Japan**
Date **1950–60**
Height **7½in (19cm)**
This surprisingly realistic animated figure is a fine representation of the giant "King Kong" – but reduced to a mere 7½ in. When the clockwork mechanism is activated, the toy walks slowly forwards, beating its chest and growling realistically as it advances. A larger, battery-operated version of this toy was also made. It is moderately rare.

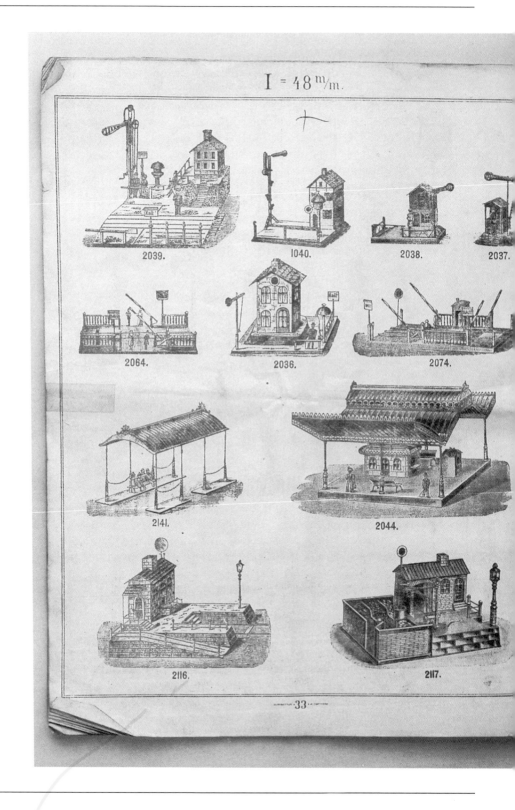

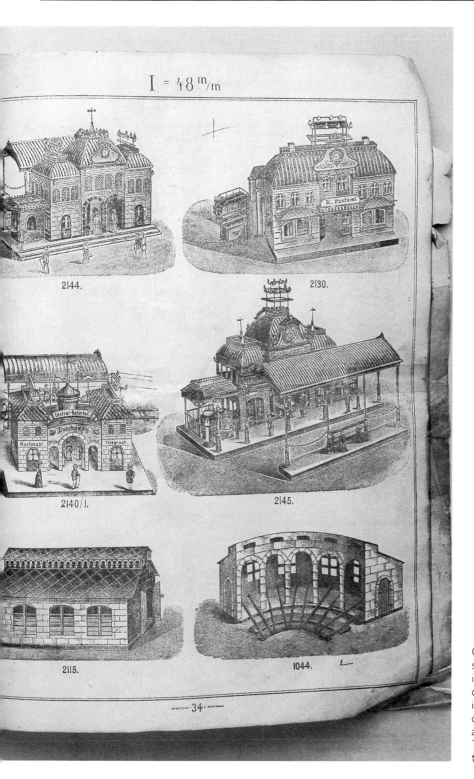

Catalogue collecting is always an interesting sideline and an excellent means of gaining information on the subject, for catalogues can often reveal some hitherto unknown information. This example illustrates some of the turn-of-the-century toy railway accessories produced by Gebrüder Märklin. They don't make model railway stations like that any more!

Clockwork Performing Clown and Dogs.
Price ... **3 6** Postage 3d.

Clockwork Singing Bird in Cage, 1/-
Postage 3d.

Clockwork Duck.
Price **10½d.** Postage 3d.

Clockwork Rabbit 8½d.
„ **Skin Rabbit** 10½d.
„ **Skin Squirrel** 10½d.
Postage 3d.

Clockwork Hen, 10½d. Clockwork Frog, 8½d.
Postage 3d. Postage 2d.

Movable Clown and Donkey.
Very Strong Clockwork Toy.
Price ... ... **2 11** Postage 3d.

Clockwork Elephant with Ball.
Price **1/4½** Postage 3d.

Clockwork Goat.
Price **10½d.** Postage 3d.

Clockwork Performing Dogs.
Price ... ... **10½d.** Postage 3d.

Clockwork Peacock.
Wags Head and Tail.
Price **10½d.** Postage 3d.

The Walking Elephant. Most Natural and Amusing.

Clockwork Cat ... **10½d.**
„ **Mice** ... **10½d.**
Postage 3d.

The Jumping Kangaroo.
Jumps with life-like movements on an inclined plane.
Price **6d.** Postage 3d.

Price **6d.** No Clockwork to get out of order. Postage 3d.

4.
BUYING AND SELLING

Before embarking on this fascinating hobby, it would be prudent to obtain as much practical experience as possible. Reading just a few of the many books that have been published on this subject will indicate the enormous range of types and makes of tin toys produced over the years. However, viewing and handling the actual toys is even better, and this practical instruction may be gained by visiting museums and toy fairs.

It may be possible to find a local collector who is willing to show you his collection and help you gain the crucial but indefinable "feel" for the different types and ages of toys. An ability to tell the good from the bad – there are many restored toys and not-too-honest dealers about unfortunately – is a valuable accomplishment, which really cannot be acquired without actually handling both the genuine article and the fake.

Whatever your chosen collecting theme – toy boats, toy cars, even toy bicycles – the obvious place to look for items is the toy fair or swap meet, and these are organized regularly all over the country – there seems to be an event almost every weekend. Tin toys do appear occasionally in antique shops and on stalls at antique fairs, while the stalls at flea markets and jumble sales and car-boot sales can often be rewarding.

You might also consider advertising in your local newspaper. Although advertising is not cheap, an announcement in the local paper that you are interested in a particular type of toy or maker often brings results.

Most British toy swap meets concentrate on diecast models (some of them quite modern), but tinplate toys are usually well represented at most events. Toy fairs are held all over the British Isles, the majority making their appearance over week-ends, though mid-week evening swapmeets are now fairly widespread.

If you become seriously interested in the hobby you might consider taking a stall at such an event. This can be great fun and will serve as an excellent introduction to fellow dealers and collectors. Almost invariably the toy collector will find that he has excess items, which may be sold or swapped at a swap meet to help towards the purchase of further toys. Do remember to keep records as the Inland Revenue may become interested! In 1987 stall rents average £10–15 a day for a 6ft (2m) table, but a stall needs to be reserved well in advance, especially at the more popular events where there could well be a waiting list!

Similar events in the United States generally offer a higher standard of goods than their British counterparts. In Paris, France, the bi-annual toy fair known as "Toymania" is considered to be the most important

A page from Gamage's 1902 catalogue illustrating just a few of the novelty toys that were made, mostly in Germany, for export to Britain.

Maker **Arnold**
Marks *Arnold* [in a banner] over a triangle
Date **1940s**
Length **13¾in (35cm)**
These three toys are typical of the early post-World War II products of the German firm Arnold. The lower two, a shunting locomotive and a coal mine, were also produced in the 1930s. Another similar

model, not illustrated, represents a life-boat travelling backwards and forwards and includes an illuminated lighthouse.

All are, basically, the same toy, with the moving part being affixed to an endless-belt clockwork mechanism. The locomotive makes its repetitive journey up and down the track until the clockwork runs down. Although a tightrope-walking clown replaces

the vehicle in the top toy, the action is the same. This is a rarer version, possibly made only in the 1950s or early 1960s. The tightrope-walker version of this group of toys is the most difficult to find. The others are more common, especially the shunting locomotive version.

Maker **Märklin**
Marks ***G.M. & Cie.*** [intertwined] in a shield
Date **1906–14**
Length **8¾in (22cm)**
Märklin made only a few cars, but, like the one pictured here, they were of the highest quality. This model has opening rear doors, nickel headlamps and a brake operating the rear wheels; the motor is clockwork. A very rare toy.

European event of its kind, while the annual London Toy Convention attracts toy enthusiasts from all over the world. The dates of these events and many others held in different parts of the world can be found in the international monthly magazine *Antique Toy World*, and European events are listed in *Collector's Gazette* (see page 142). Their informative text and advertisements help the collector to keep pace with prices and with items in especial demand as well as providing a mine of interesting information on the subject.

Toy values vary widely, from week to week and from place to place – even the top auctioneers appear incapable of accurately forecasting the amounts many of the toys they handle are expected to raise, judging by the estimates printed in their catalogues. International rates of exchange can make a difference, of course, but only by continually studying auction prices and the price guides that appear on the market (even though these are usually out of date by the time they appear in the shops) will you keep in touch with current prices.

Many prices depend on the country of origin. German collectors, for instance, set the prices paid for Märklin products. They are particularly keen to buy the products of this famous manufacturer. Lionel trains, beloved by the Americans, will, for nostalgic reasons, naturally tend to be more desirable in the United States; in Britain there is little interest in Lionel trains. Early classical toys in a good state of preservation raise the highest prices, and most of these were made in Germany.

Penny toys from the David Pressland collection – just a few of the hundreds of different types that were manufactured. This is a splendid collection, which, David Pressland declares, is "not the largest in the world, by any means". To build up such a collection today would be both difficult and costly. *Photograph Jack Tempest*

5.
LOOKING AFTER YOUR COLLECTION

The best possible condition in which a toy can have survived the years is described as "mint and boxed". The appearance of such a toy should be perfect, just as it was the day it left the factory where it was made. The box is an added bonus and should be well looked after – definitely never thrown away. If the toy is to be displayed in a showcase, the box should be safely stored away where it cannot be damaged. Many of the cartons in which toys were sold have interesting, colourful decoration, and they often bear labels that are evocative of the period when the toy was manufactured as well as giving additional information about place of manufacture, patents applied for and so on.

Not all toys were issued with boxes or, as is more probable, the original packing has gone astray. The toy can still, however, be described as "mint". It may have been particularly well cared for or it may have been a "Sunday toy" belonging to a strict Victorian or Edwardian family, in which toys could be enjoyed quietly only after a visit to church. The premature death of a child often led the grieving parents to preserve the toys.

Such pristine examples are far from easy to find, and most collectors have to make do with second best. These are toys that are in a satisfactory condition and have suffered little at the hands of careless children. Such toys are generally quite pleasing in appearance and largely free from damage, with no more than the odd minor abrasion. There are, of course, very well-behaved children who are perfectly capable of leaving their toys in near perfect condition, but there is no doubt that tin toys would not be as rare as they are if every child was careful.

Toys in poor condition can be of interest only to a collector if they are real rarities, when few or even no other examples are known to exist. However they may also be wanted if they are worth restoration or if they can be used as a source of spare parts to repair other toys.

Restoring old toys is a task that must not be undertaken lightly and that is best left to experts who have had plenty of experience. Old toys are too precious to be experimented upon by amateurs. A certain amount of engineering expertise is essential, and even simple soldering can lead to disaster if the repair is attempted in a way that allows the heat to discolour or burn the lithography on the opposite side of the metal. Amateurs are liable to do this, just as they may tend to use modern adhesives, which could prove a severe hindrance to future restorers who

A clockwork billiard player with six billiard balls, made by Günthermann c.1906.

find them practically impossible to remove. Evidence of amateur repairs will definitely reduce the interest of a prospective purchaser.

Clockwork springs often need repairing, which is not, in itself, a difficult task. However, replacing the original spring by a weaker one can reduce the efficiency of the toy, just as the use of a more powerful spring may cause damage to gears by stripping off the teeth and leading to further, more expensive, repairs. If a break occurs near either end of a spring, it can be refixed without having any very noticeable effect on the operation of the toy. Shortening a spring too much will, of course, lead to a definite loss of power and a briefer performance. The "piano-wire" springs, wound onto a cylinder and found in many toys, are rarely found to break, although many of these mechanisms were cheaply made and are more trouble than they are worth to repair when they do go wrong, which usually happens when inferior materials were combined with poor design.

Repainting toys rarely proves successful, and it is best to leave them in the condition in which they were found. It is possible to imitate the original effect of toys that were hand painted, but it is better to leave this to a specialist. Lithographed toys require extra-skilled attention, and the

Maker **Martin**
Marks *F.M.*
Date **1890**
Height **4in (10cm)**
Animals have always been favourite subjects for imitation by toy makers, and this tin rabbit – *le lapin vivant* – was made by Fernand Martin. The rabbit has a fly-wheel mechanism that causes it to move its paws and raise its ears as it trundles forwards.

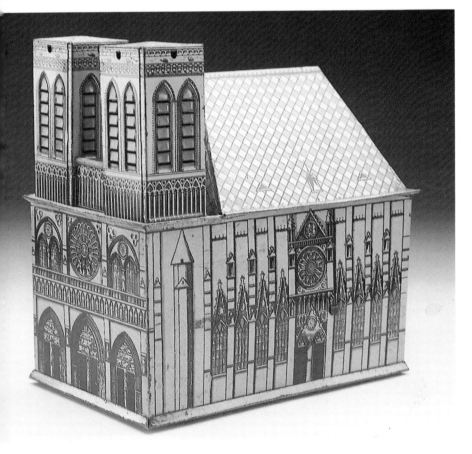

ABOVE
Maker **Bing**
Marks *G.B.N.* in a diamond
Date **1900s**
Length **3ft 3in (1m)**
This model of a torpedo boat has been fully restored from an incomplete survivor of the 1900s. One of the funnels, the masts and guns have been faithfully copied. The large clockwork motor works as well as it ever did and is in excellent condition. Not the rarest of tinplate boats, but, nevertheless, difficult to find.

LEFT
Maker **Unknown German**
Marks *Made in Germany*
Date **Late 1920s–1930s**
Length **6¼in (16cm)**; width **4in (10cm)**
An unusual tinplate toy – a model of Notre-Dame Cathedral, Paris. When the handle at the rear is wound, a series of musical chords is produced from the simple organ mechanism within. The lithography is extremely detailed. Other similar "cathedral" toys of varying appearance may be found, but they are not common.

item itself must be important enough to warrant the time, trouble and expense involved.

Gaining access to the mechanism of tin toys often means disassembling the toy, and great care must be taken in opening – and eventually closing – the tinplate clips that hold it together in order not to break them off. The more frequently they are opened and closed the weaker they become, and, obviously, someone may have opened them before you. Always work slowly as you unfold and close them up, taking particular care not to scratch the surrounding paintwork.

Rusty mechanisms can be treated with small quantities of a proprietary rust remover, which will usually disperse both rust and dirt. Try to clean clockwork mechanisms as thoroughly as possible – ideally, the motor should be taken to pieces, but the trouble of gaining access to its may be too much, especially if the tabs on the toy's body appear likely to snap off. Fortunatley, the majority of toy mechanisms are quite robust in their simplicity and do not generally require the careful treatment demanded by watch and clock movements. When the clogging dirt has been cleaned out, touch the moving pinions with a drop of oil. Only a drop – keep the mechanism covered in oil and it will quickly attract more dirt and fluff.

Some knowledge of electrics will come in useful if you are going to tackle repairs to battery toys. The battery compartments of many of these toys are found to have been eaten away by corrosion caused by previous owners failing to remove batteries when they put the toy away. Repairs depend on the state of the damage, which can often be quite critical. As prevention is always better than cure, it is wise to remove the batteries from these toys each time they are put away.

Loose connections, a common problem in battery toys, can be a simple soldering operation – unless they are in an inaccessible place. Getting inside these toys is usually, once again, a matter of undoing tinplate tabs. With the automata type the figures are often finished in fabric clothing, which will have to be removed. The fabric will generally pull away from the tinplate underneath but do take care. It can be replaced by using a latex fabric adhesive, which will disappear without trace on drying.

Faulty electric motors and smoke generating units may need to be replaced, and these can be obtained only from similar broken models in which these parts may be still intact. When smoking models cease to emit smoke, check to see if the apertures are blocked – gently blowing out any obstruction may do the trick. Fresh batteries are often a cure, too. A model that fails to work after having been in storage for a time may need a little gentle encouragement, and you should work the moving parts very gently indeed after inserting fresh batteries.

A more serious problem arises if any of the gears are suffering from metal fatigue, which is often the case if they have been made from a diecast metal. Again, "borrowing" from broken models may be the only solution. Plastic gears sometimes run loose on their spindles, and they

Maker **Masutoku Toy Factory**
Marks *MT* [in a diamond] *Made in Japan*
Date **1960s**
Height **8in (21cm)**

"Bubble Bear" is a typical Japanese battery toy made by the Masutoku Toy Factory in Tokyo during the 1950s. When it is switched on, the bear moves its lighted pipe away from its mouth and emits a shower of detergent bubbles. It then replaces the pipe and so on, repeating the action until it is switched off or runs out of bubbles. Detergent fluid placed in the bear's mouth is picked up in a fine film by a small loop of wire, which is then moved in front of a thin jet of air, which forms and blows out the bubbles. This is one of the more commonly found battery toys.

may be repaired by the careful application of a little super glue – probably the only time the use of a modern adhesive can be recommended.

Looking after a collection of tin toys depends, of course, on the facilities that are available in your home. Obviously, the ideal arrangement would be to set them all out in display cabinets so they can be shown off to their advantage. Never place a toy in strong sunlight because this can eventually cause the colours to fade. Similarly, an electrically illuminated showcase could prove detrimental, not so much from the actual light but from the heat of the bulb. Make sure that any items are kept away from the bulb source and that the cabinet is ventilated.

Tin, of course, rusts. It is essential that no tin toy is kept in a bathroom or kitchen, for once tin has rusted externally nothing can be done. If the rust has affected the tin internally, use soft wire wool or a wire brush to treat it; once rust becomes established it will gradually eat through the metal destroying both the object itself and the image lithographed on it.

Although dents may be smoothed out – perhaps with a wooden spoon – the pressure that caused the dent will, in all likelihood, have stretched the metal, and the toy can never be restored to its original shape. Whenever you have to transport any of your toys, wrap them in several sheets of newspaper to protect them.

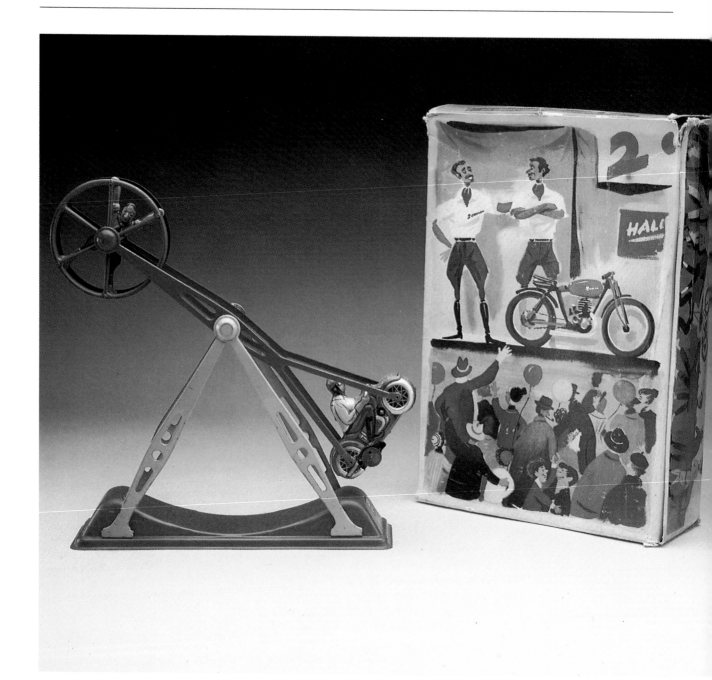

Maker **Arnold**

Marks *Arnold* [in a banner] over a triangle

Date **1960s**

Length **(of base) 8¾in (22cm)**

This toy by the West German firm of Arnold represents a hair-raising fairground stunt incorporating a motorcycle counterbalanced by a man in a revolving wheel. The drive mechanism, which is clockwork, is in the bike, and it gives enough power to cause the bike to "loop the loop", emitting sparks from its exhaust as it goes. This ingenious toy occasionally turns up on stalls at toy fairs.

INTERNATIONAL TOY MANUFACTURERS

Richard & Karl (Carl) Adam
Königsberg, East Prussia
Founded c. 1895
Manufactured animated tin toys.
Trademark: Dancing lady on a globe

Alemanni
Milan, Italy
Founded in 1908 by Leonida Alemanni
Made a variety of small tinplate toys,
    including an interesting range of toy
    vehicles.
Trademark: *LAC*

Alga
Vittsjo, Sweden
Specialized in the manufacture of toy
    steam engines.
Trademark: *Alga* on a circle

Alps Shoji Ltd
Tokyo, Japan
Founded in 1948
Maker of many colourful tinplate
    novelty toys, both clockwork and
    battery operated.
Trademark: Mountain logo with *Alps*

Althof, Bergmann & Co.
New York, U.S.A.
Founded in 1867
Originally in business as jobbers, the
    company entered the toy trade in
    1874, commissioning toys and
    possibly manufacturing some. One
    of first U.S. companies to make
    carpet trains.
Trademark: *A.B.C.* (registered in 1881)

American Flyer
Chicago, U.S.A.
Founded in 1907
Prolific manufacturers of toy trains in
    both cast iron and tinplate; also
    made the unsuccessful "British
    Flyer" for the British market.
Trademark: *American Flyer*

Arnold
Nuremberg, Germany
Founded in 1906 by Karl Arnold
Pioneered the sparking flint toy and
    produced a large range of novelty
    toys both before and after World
    War II.
Trademarks: *Arnold* and *Rapido* (on
    trains during 1960s)

Asahi Toy Co.
Tokyo, Japan
Founded in 1950
Produced many toys with novelty
    actions.
Trademark: Father Christmas carrying
    a sack marked *A.T.C.*

Asakusa Toy Ltd
Tokyo, Japan
Founded in 1950
Manufactured many colourfully
    lithographed tinplate novelty toys.
Trademark: A stylized dog's face, with
    A.I. forming the eyes

Automatic Toy Works
New York, U.S.A.
Founded in 1868 by Robert J. Clay
An early U.S. manufacturer of
    clockwork toys.

Bandai
Tokyo, Japan
Founded in 1950
Produced many splendid tinplate toys,
    including an excellent range of toy
    cars.
Trademark: Gothic *B* within a *C*

Bassett-Lowke Ltd
Northampton, England
Founded in 1899 by Wenman J.
    Bassett-Lowke
Originally worked in conjunction with
    Bing and Carette (*qq.v.*) making
    model railways and some boats; later
    became one of leading British
    companies making toy trains.
Trademark: *Lowko*

Bell
Milan, Italy
Founded in 1919 by Vittorio Belloni
Made many small mechanical tin toys;
    after World War II produced a
    variety of novelty cars and toys.

Betal Toys
England
Founded c.1984.
Trade name of J. H. Glasman, Ltd, London.
    Marketed clockwork tinplate trains,
    trolley buses, and buses. Also diecast
    toys and other play things.
Trademark: *Betal*

Biller
Nuremberg, Germany
Founded in 1937 by Hans Biller
Biller, an engineer with Bing (*q.v.*),
   made toy railways and novelties,
   and, after World War II, helicopters
   and trains.
Trademark: A large *B* with silhouette of
key for clockwork mechanism

Gebrüder Bing
Nuremberg, Germany
Founded in 1863 or 1865 by Ignaz and
   Adolf Bing
A prolific manufacturer of toys
   specializing in boats, cars and trains.
   Taken over by Bub (*q.v.*) in 1933.
Trademark: Varied over the years but
   usually incorporated the letters
   G.B.N. (until World War I) and *B.W.*
   (between 1917 and 1932)

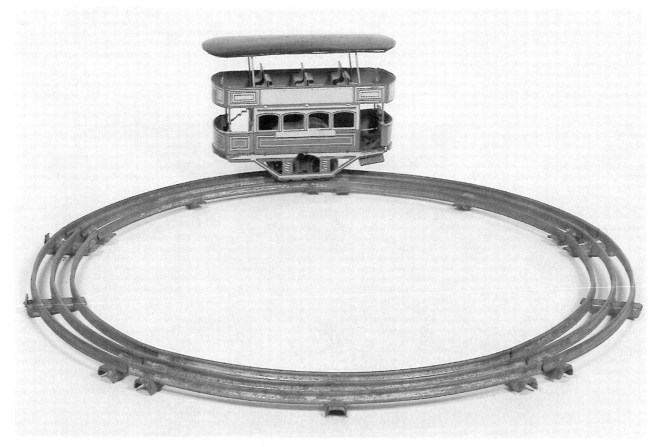

ABOVE
Maker **Bing**
Marks **G.B.N. [in a diamond]**
Date **1900s**
Length **6¼in (16cm)**
Powered by electricity, this Bing gauge I
tram is a rare toy. Tram models have a
novelty appeal of their own, which is greatly
appreciated by collectors. *Sotheby's*

Maker **Blomer & Schüler**
Marks **[Elephant trademark]**
Date **1930s**
Length **5in (13cm)**
The German firm Blomer & Schüler
specialized in producing mechanical tinplate
animals – its first toy was a walking elephant,
and the company adopted this as its
trademark. Here is a walking horse

complete with German soldier – all in
tinplate except for the soldier's head. The
horse may look a little short in the legs, but it
walks well. Such a toy would be quite
difficult to obtain nowadays.

Bird & Sons
Birmingham, England
Founded in 1870s by Alfred Bird
Produced tinplate toys during the
1930s.
Trademark: A weathervane

Blomer & Schüler
Nuremberg, Germany
Founded c.1919
Started by making clockwork
mechanisms but branched out into
the novelty toy business.
Trademark: Elephant with *B. & S.*

Bolz
Zirndorf, Germany
Founded in 1875 by Lorenz Bolz
Manufactured humming tops and
seaside toys (buckets and spades,
etc.) as well as a few novelty toys.
Trademark: *L.B.Z.* and *Elbezet*

Bonnet et Cie
Paris, France
Founded in 1912
Victor Bonnet took over Fernand
Martin's factory (*q.v.*) in 1912 and
made various clockwork novelties
and trucks, fire-engines, etc.
Trademark: *V.B.* or *Vebe*

 VéBé

Bowman Models Ltd
Dereham, England
Founded in 1923 by G. Bowman
Jenkins
Manufactured gauge O live steam
locomotives.
Trademark: Bow and arrow

Braglia
Milan, Italy
Founded in 1913 by Roberto Braglia
Made many small toys of various types
including airplane construction sets;
after World War II made gauge O
trains.

Georg Brandstätter
Zirndorf, Germany
Founded in 1877 by Andreas
Brandstätter

Manufactured tinplate toys and
perambulators.
Trademark: *Geobra*

Brianne
Paris, France
Founded c.1889
Made tinplate model railway stations,
large and small, also a "giant" train;
imported Bing and Carette (*qq.v.*)
toy railways into France.

Brimtoy Ltd
London, England
Founded before 1914
Manufacturer of cheap train sets and
road vehicles; amalgamated with
Wells (*q.v.*).
Trademark: Nelson's Column

William Britain
London, England
Founded mid-19th century
Produced mechanical toys similar in
style to those of Fernand Martin
(*q.v.*) but later devoted production
to lead figures and military items.
Trademark: *W. Britain* (also in form of
signature on box labels)

British Flyer *see* American Flyer

George W. Brown & Co.
Connecticut, U.S.A.
Founded in 1856
One of leading toy makers in the
United States, producing a great
variety of clockwork toys from
novelty figures to boats.
Trademark: the company name
printed on a paper label

Bub
Nuremberg, Germany
Founded in 1851 by Karl Bub
Made a variety of tinplate toys, some
with clockwork mechanisms; took
over Bing in 1933.

Trademark: A windmill with *K.B.N* or
K.B.; used *B.W.* with *K.B.* after 1933

mechanism): Spruce fir tree

A. Bucherer & Co.
Diepoldsan, Switzerland
Founded in 1945
Made model railways.
Trademark: *Buco*

Bühler
Triberg and Nuremberg, Germany
Founded in 1860 by the Bühler
brothers
Supplied clockwork mechanisms to toy
manufacturers.
Trademark (stamped on key or

Burnett Ltd
Birmingham and London, England
Founded 1900–10
Made interesting tinplate road vehicles;
taken over by Chad Valley (*q.v.*).
Trademark: includes *London* after
October 1914; a circle containing St
George and dragon. Also *Ubilda*

Butcher & Sons Ltd
London, England
Founded c.1920
Made toy cars and construction kits.
Trademark: *Primus Engineering*

Camtoys
England
Founded in 1940s or 1950s
Made cheap, rather poor quality, tinplate toy lorries.
Trademark: *Camtoy*

Ettore Cardini Co.
Omegna, Italy
Founded in 1922
Made good quality tin toys – road vehicles, planes, etc. – until its closure in 1928.
Trademark: A crest incorporating *Cardini*; winged arrow in circular logo; car wheels were marked *Pirelli-cord*

ABOVE LEFT
Maker **A. Bucherer**
Marks **None**
Date *c.*1920
Height **7¾in (20cm)**
These two character dolls may well be classed as tinplate toys for they have articulated metal bodies. They are two of a series of character figures produced by the Swiss manufacturer A. Bucherer during the 1920s. Some of the figures, which have moulded composition heads, hands and feet, are of well-known personalities, but others are of cartoon characters, and the photograph shows "Mama Katzenjammer" and "Der Captain" from the American comic strip "The Captain and the Kids" (sometimes known as "The Katzenjammer Kids"). Many of these figures are found unclothed and in boxes bearing art shop labels, suggesting that they were often supplied as artists' lay figures. Such toys are difficult to find.

ABOVE
Maker **Brimtoy (Wells)**
Marks *Brimtoy Made in England*
Date **Early 1960s**
Length **7½in (19cm)**
The two figures operating the railway truck are characters from the Walt Disney animated movie *Cinderella*. The mice – Gus and Jaq – are made of composition, but the rest of the toy is tinplate and powered by clockwork. Manufactured by Brimtoy in the early 1960s, the toy was nicely presented in a colourful box, complete with a circle of track. Brimtoy also made a similar set featuring Mickey Mouse and Minnie, but the *Cinderella* set is possibly rarer. A fairly rare toy, made rarer by its additional appeal to collectors of Disneyana.
Courtesy Chester Toy and Doll Museum

A fine model steam boat by Carette, made not long before the outbreak of World War I. The model seen here was 21½in (55cm) long, but other versions, 25½in (65cm) and 29½in (75cm) long, were also available.

Carette
Nuremberg, Germany
Founded in 1886 by Georges Carette
Made steam toys, mechanical tin cars, trams, aircraft, boats and railways.
Trademark: Various designs incorporating *G.C.* or *G.C. & Cie*

Carlisle & Finch
Cincinatti, Ohio, U.S.A.
Founded in 1894 by Robert S. Finch and Morton Carlisle
Made model railways and electric-powered streetcars.

Carpenter
Westchester, New York, U.S.A.
Founded in 1844 by Francis W. Harrington Carpenter
Early U.S. manufacturer of toys.
Trademark: sometimes used *XL*

Centola
Bologna, Italy
Founded in 1934
Manufactured a variety of toys, including tinplate cars.

Trademark: *F.C.R.* after 1947, when the company moved to Roseto

Chad Valley
Birmingham, England
Founded in 1887 by Joseph Johnson
Achieved fame for tinplate toys – mainly cars and buses – in the 1930s; also made soft toys; took over Burnett (*q.v.*).
Trademark: *Chad Valley* or *Ubilda* (on constructional sets after take-over of Burnett)

Chein
Harrison, New Jersey, and Burlington, Philadelphia, U.S.A.
Founded c.1903 by Julius Chein
Manufactured tinplate toy vehicles and character toys; pioneered use of lithography.

C.I.J. (Compagnie Industrielle du Jouet)
Paris, France
Founded c.1920
Made top quality model cars, including an Alfa Romeo P2; took over André Citroën Toys (*q.v.*) in 1936.
Trademark: *CIJ*

André Citroën
Briare, France

Started production in 1923
Made models of Citroën cars to promote the real thing; the very detailed tinplate toys were made by C.I.J. from 1936.
Trademark: *Automobile Mécanique André Citroën*

Codeg *see* Cowan de Groot Ltd

Congost
Barcelona, Spain
Made animated tinplate toys.
Trademark: *Congost*

Cowan de Groot Ltd
England
Produced simple tinplate toys (cash registers, etc.); also a tinplate and plastic "Dalek".
Trademark: *Codeg*

Cragstan
U.S.A.
Founded c.1955
Distributor of a wide variety of toys, including many Japanese-made items.
Trademark: *Cragstan* appeared on toys made by a variety of manufacturers

Dae Jin Industrial Co.
South Korea
Founded in 1955
Produced colourfully lithographed novelty and fantasy toys and some toy cars.
Trademark: *Jamina*

Decamps
Paris, France
Founded in 1847 by H. E. Decamps
Made toys tending towards the quality

of automata such as mechanical, skin-covered animals with novelty actions.

Johann Distler
Nuremberg, Germany
Founded in 1900
Famed for penny toys and a range of toy cars and trains; eventually taken over by Trix.
Trademark: *J.D.* on a thistle (*distler* is German for "thistle") or *J.D.N.* on a globe; after World War II *Distler*

A Distler toy bus made *c*.1920. The passengers at the windows are lithographed, and the mechanism is clockwork.

Doll & Cie
Nuremberg, Germany
Founded in 1898 by J. Sondheim and Peter Doll
Made steam engines and other novelty toys; taken over by Fleischmann (*q.v.*) in 1938.
Trademark: *D.C.* intertwined in an oval

Dorfan Co.
Newark, New Jersey, U.S.A.
Founded in 1924
Emigrant relatives of Josef Kraus (*q.v.*) manufactured model railways, rearranging Kraus's trademark, *Fandor*, for their own tradename.
Trademark: *Dorfan*

Dunbee-Combex-Marx
England
Became the world's largest manufacturer of toys by taking over Schuco, Marx and Lines Brothers (*qq.v.*), but went bankrupt in 1980.

Dux (Markes & Co.)
Lüdenscheidt, Germany
Founded in 1904 by Carl Markes
Better known by its tradename "Dux", Markes & Co. specialized in model car and aircraft construction kits.
Trademark: *Dux*

Hans Eberl
Nuremberg, Germany
Founded *c*.1900 by Hans Eberl
Produced novelty toys – e.g., walking peacocks – and cars.
Trademark: *H.E.N.*; also a clown in a circle with *Ebo Hui Hui* (or *Oi Oi*)

Gebrüder Einfalt
Nuremberg, Germany
Founded in 1922 by Georg and Johann Einfalt
Produced a wide range of novelty toys –

boxing kangaroos, climbing monkeys – and road vehicles.
Trademark: Originally *G.E.N.*; after 1935 *Technofix*

Elastolin *see* O. & M. Hausser

Essdee
Germany
Founded *c*.1920
Tin toys with the trademark of a running boy carrying a box marked *Essdee* may have been manufactured by Distler (*q.v.*)

Ever Ready
London, England
Although best known as manufacturers of dry batteries, the company produced a tinplate, battery-powered model of a London Underground train in 1953.
Trademark: *Ever Ready*

F.R.
Rome, Italy
Founded in early 20th century

Produced a range of toy cars in lithographed tinplate.

Faivre
Paris, France
Founded in 1860 by Edmond Faivre
Specialized in tinplate clockwork toys, mainly trains but also some cars.
Trademark: *F.V.*

J. Falk
Nuremberg, Germany
Founded in 1897 by Joseph Falk
Made steam toys and magic lanterns.
Trademark: Lighthouse and *J.F.* in an oval or *Falk*

James Fallows
Philadelphia, U.S.A.
Founded in 1880
Manufactured model Mississippi-type river boats and horse-drawn vehicles; *see also* Francis, Field & Francis.
Trademark: *IXL* ("I excel")

Georg Fischer
Nuremberg, Germany
Founded in 1903 by Georg Fischer
Made simple mechanical tinplate toys, many of fascinating actions.
Trademark: *G.F.* intertwined

Gustav Fischer
Zöblitz, Germany
Manufactured sheet-metal tin toys.
Trademark: *Efzet* or stylized crowned fish

H. Fischer & Co.
Nuremberg, Germany
Founded in 1908 by Henry Fischer
Manufactured a variety of tinplate toys, including cars, and various animated toys such as the "Toonerville Trolley" of comic-strip fame.
Trademark: A fish or a knight in armour

Gebrüder Fleischmann
Nuremberg, Germany
Founded in 1887 by Jean Fleischmann
Manufactured a wide range of toys, especially boats and magnetic floating toys; later produced model trains.
Trademark: *G.F.N.* in a triangle

Förtner & Haffner
Nuremberg, Germany
Founded in early 1920s by Andreas Förtner and Johannes Haffner
Made tin soldier "flats" and sundry small novelties; taken over by Stephan Bing in 1927 and eventually became Trix (*q.v.*).
Trademark: *Anfoe*

J.E. Fournereau
Seine-et-Oise, France
Founded in 1928
Made simple but good quality scale model railways; based on the firm of Marescot (*q.v.*), it became J.F.J. in 1951 but closed in 1958.

Francis, Field & Francis
Philadelphia, U.S.A.

Founded *c.*1838
Made housewares and simple tin toys; in 1870 James Fallows (*q.v.*) joined the company as foreman, and the company took his name in 1880s.
Trademark: company name

Fuchs & Co.
Nuremberg, Germany
Produced animated tin toys and musical instruments.
Trademark: *Fuchs* and a fox's head in a circle

Fuchs
Zirndorf, Germany
Founded in 1919 by Martin Fuchs
In addition to humming tops, the company made a variety of small toys including carousels.
Trademark: *M.F.Z.*

Gakken
Tokyo, Japan
Founded after World War II
Manufactured novelty toys.
Trademark: *Gakken*

Gama *see* Mangold

Garlick & Co.
Paterson, New Jersey, U.S.A.
Founded *c.*1885 by John Garlick
Made live steam model locomotives.

Geyper S.A. Indestrias
Valencia, Spain
Made tinplate toy motor cars.

Gilbert & Co.
New Haven, Connecticut, U.S.A.
Founded in 1909 by A. C. Gilbert
Manufactured conjuring sets and construction kits ("Erector"). Took over American Flyer (*q.v.*) in 1938.

Maker **Einfalt**
Marks *Technofix*
Date **1950s**
Length **17¾in (45cm)**

Track toys are always fascinating and often intriguingly ingenious. Their only drawback is that they take up rather a lot of space to display. They have been made for a number of years, but the most compact versions appeared just after World War II, made by the West German firm Gebrüder Einfalt under the tradename Technofix. The toy illustrated is called "Cable Car". When the clockwork mechanism is wound up, the two tiny cable cars travel up and down the mountain, while, at the same time, a couple of little motor cars journey around the encircling road. On entering the tunnel, each car is mysteriously elevated to the higher road level, ready to freewheel downhill. The excellently coloured lithography adds interest. The popularity of these toys with collectors is increasing, and they are now quite difficult to find. *Private collection*

Gioia
Florence, Italy
Founded in 1866 by Giacomo Gioia
Produced metalware originally, but
    began toy making in 1890, producing
    excellent model road vehicles.

Girard Model Works Inc
Girard, Pennsylvania, U.S.A.
Manufactured tinplate toys that were
    distributed by Louis Marx.

Glud & Marstrand
Copenhagen, Denmark
Manufactured tinplate horse-drawn
    pull toys and novelties.
Trademark: *Danske Legetoejs
    Industri, København*

Götz & Son
Furth, Germany
Founded in 1920 by Christian Götz
Produced a variety of tinplate toys.
Trademark: *Göso* usually in an
    ornamental circle

Greppert & Kelch (Gundka-Werke)
Brandenburg, Germany
Founded c.1900
Produced many small tinplate toys,
    often in the style of Lehmann (*q.v.*).
Trademark: *G. & K.* in a hexagon

Günthermann
Nuremberg, Germany
Founded in 1877 by Siegfried
    Günthermann
Manufactured a wide range of toys
    including horse-drawn vehicles, cars
    and aircraft.
Trademark: *S.G.*; between 1903 and
    1920 sometimes incorporated

initials *A.W.* (for Adolf Weigel who
married Günthermann's widow in
1890)

Gutmann
Paris, France
Founded by Mery Gutmann
Produced a variety of tin toys,
    including cars with "piano-wire"
    clockwork mechanisms; *see also*
    S.F.A.
Trademark: *Memo*

Hafner Manufacturing Co.
Chicago, U.S.A.
Founded in 1901 by W. F. Hafner
Made tinplate toy cars with clockwork
    mechanisms. Eventually taken over
    by Marx.
Trademark: *New York Flyer*

Haji *see* Mansei Toy Company

Emil Hausmann
Nuremberg, Germany
Manufactured tinplate novelty toys,
    trains and steam engines; also
    acted as the wholesaler of the
    products of such manufacturers as
    Arnold, Bub, Doll, Fleischmann
    and Plank.
Trademark: *E.H.N.* and *E.H.A.*

O. & M. Hausser
Ludwigsburg, Germany
Founded in 1904 by Otto and Max
    Hausser
Specialized in well-made tinplate
    military vehicles; also made
    composition toy figures under the
    tradename *Elastolin*.
Trademarks: *O.M.H.L.* in a diamond
    and gable-end of a house (formed

from letters L. H.) in a circle

Heller & Schiller
Obersleutensdorf, Germany (now
    Czechoslovakia)
Founded c.1939
Manufactured small tinplate items –
    e.g., buckets and spades – and also
    trams, trains, aircraft and cars.
Trademark: *Husch*

Hess
Nuremberg, Germany
Founded in 1826 by Mattheus
    (Mathias) Hess
Originally manufactured toy trains but
    later introduced its fly-wheel driven
    "Hessmobile" range of toy cars,
    identifiable from starting handle
    used to wind up friction mechanism.
Trademark: *J and L* in an *H*; *Hessmobil*

Hoch & Beckmann
Nuremberg, Germany
Founded c.1890
Made a variety of tinplate toys, many
    distributed by Moko (*see* Kohnstam).
Trademark: none usually used

Hodge Manufacturing Co.
New York, U.S.A.
Founded in 1931
Made tinplate electric toy trains.
Trademark: *Tom Thumb Line*

Höfler
Fürth, Germany
Founded in 1938
Produced tinplate clockwork toys just
    before and after World War II.
Trademark: *J above H* in a cloverleaf

Maker **Hess**
Marks *J.L.H.* monogram
Date *c.*1915
Length **(largest ship) 8in (21cm)**
A convoy of carpet toy boats made in Germany by Hess. The large vessel, the flagship of the fleet, is fitted with a clockwork motor powerful enough to tow the other ships along. An interesting toy – or toys – which is reasonably rare, especially in its complete form. *Sotheby's*

Horikawa Toys
Tokyo, Japan
Founded in 1959
Manufactured many typical post-World War II toys.
Trademark: *S.H.* in a diamond

Hornby
Liverpool, England
Founded in 1901 by Frank Hornby
Best known for production of Meccano and toy trains; introduced Dinky toys in 1933 and produced vast range of toy road vehicles; branches in France and the United States.
Trademark: *Meccano*

Howard Electric Novelty Co.
New York, U.S.A.
Founded c.1904
Specialized in the manufacture of electric model railways.

Hull & Stafford
Clinton, Connecticut, U.S.A.
Founded c.1860
Originally Hull & Wright, manufactured a variety of mechanical toys including horse-drawn vehicles.

Ichiko Kogyo Co. Ltd
Tokyo, Japan
Made tin toys of all kinds but specialized in motor cars.
Trademark: *PU*

Inco-Giochi (Industria Costruzione Giocattoli)
Turin, Italy
Founded in 1946
Made mechanical toys including trams, animals, ships and novelties.

Ingap (Industria Nazionale Giocattoli Automatici Padua)
Padua, Italy
Founded in 1919
The largest toy-making company in Italy; manufactured a vast range of metal toys.
Trademark: *I.N.G.A.P.*

Ingat (Industria Nazionale Giocatelli e Affini Torino)
Turin, Italy
Founded in 1947
A short-lived company manufacturing toy road vehicles.
Trademark: Lion's head

Issmayer
Nuremberg, Germany
Founded in 1861 by Johann Andreas Issmayer
Started by making novelty toys and children's cooking ranges; later made toy trains.
Trademark: *J.A.J.* on a winged wheel

Ives
Plymouth, Connecticut, U.S.A.
Founded in 1868 by Edward R. Ives
Manufactured cast-iron and tinplate
mechanical toys; later made toy
trains; became Ives, Blakeslee & Co.
in 1872 but was taken over by Lionel
(*q.v.*) in late 1920s.
Trademark: *I.B. & Co.* after 1872;
I.M.C. (Ives Manufacturing Co.)

Jensen Manufacturing Co. Inc.
Jeanette, Pennsylvania, U.S.A.
Founded c.1930
Made model steam engines.

J.E.P. (Jouets en Paris)
Paris, France
Founded (as S.I.F. (Société Industrielle
de Ferblanterie)) in 1899
Renamed Jouets de Paris in 1928 and
Jouets en Paris in 1932;
manufactured trains, boats,
submarines and cars.
Trademark: *JEP*

J.M.L.
Lyons, Paris
Founded c.1930 by M. Magnien
Specialized in the manufacture of toy
road vehicles.
Trademark: *J.M.L.* in an oval.

Jouef
France
Founded in late 19th century
Originally made cooking pans, pipes
and toys, turning, after World War I,
to mechanical and electrical toys.
Trademark: *Jouef* in a diamond

Joustra (Jouets de Strasbourg)
Strasbourg-Neudorf, France
Founded in 1935 by Guillaume Marx
Manufactured mechanical tinplate
toys.
Trademark: *Joustra*

Jubb Ltd
Sheffield, England
Founded in 1915
Made model steam locomotives and
stationary engines.

J.Y.E. (Juguettes y Estuches)
Ibi, Spain
Founded in 1940
Manufactured a variety of tin toys.
Trademark: *J.Y.E.* in a circle

Kanto Toys
Tokyo, Japan
Founded c.1950
Made many colourfully lithographed
tinplate novelty toys with clockwork
mechanisms in the 1960s.

Keim & Co.
Nuremberg, Germany
Made cheap clockwork trains; took
over Kraus & Co. in 1937 and in
1938 bought out Wilhelm Krauss
(*q.v.*).
Trademark: Stylized *K* or *Keim*

Georg Kellermann & Co.
Nuremberg, Germany
Founded in 1910 by Georg
Kellermann
Specialized in the production of penny
toys; later made simple mechanical
toys, some with clockwork
mechanisms.
Trademark: *C.K.O* or *K.C.O.*, the *C*
partly surrounding the cypher

Kienberger & Co.
Nuremberg, Germany
Founded in 1910 by Hubert Kienberger
Made clockwork toys; Georg Levy
(*q.v.*) joined the company soon after
its formation.

Trademark: *Huki*; also *Ki. Co.* in an
alarm clock

Kindler & Briel
Böblingen, Germany
Founded in 1865
Early toys were made from wood as
well as tinplate; later made tinplate
railway accessories.
Trademark: *Kibri* or Father Christmas
carrying a sack of toys

Kingsbury
New Hampshire, U.S.A.
Founded in 1888 by James Wilkins
(*q.v.*)
Wilkins' toy company was bought by
Harry Thayer Kingsbury in 1895 and
the name changed to Kingsbury in
1919; manufactured mechanical
toys.
Trademark: *Kingsbury*

Maker **Krauss**
Marks **W.K.**
Date **Early 1930s**
Height **9in (23cm)**
On the continent of Europe this type of
Ferris wheel is referred to as a "Russian
carousel". This delightfully decorated
example is designed to be turned by hand
or to be driven by a model steam engine.
These fairground toys, with their evocative
lithography, are always in demand and,
therefore, not all that easy to find.

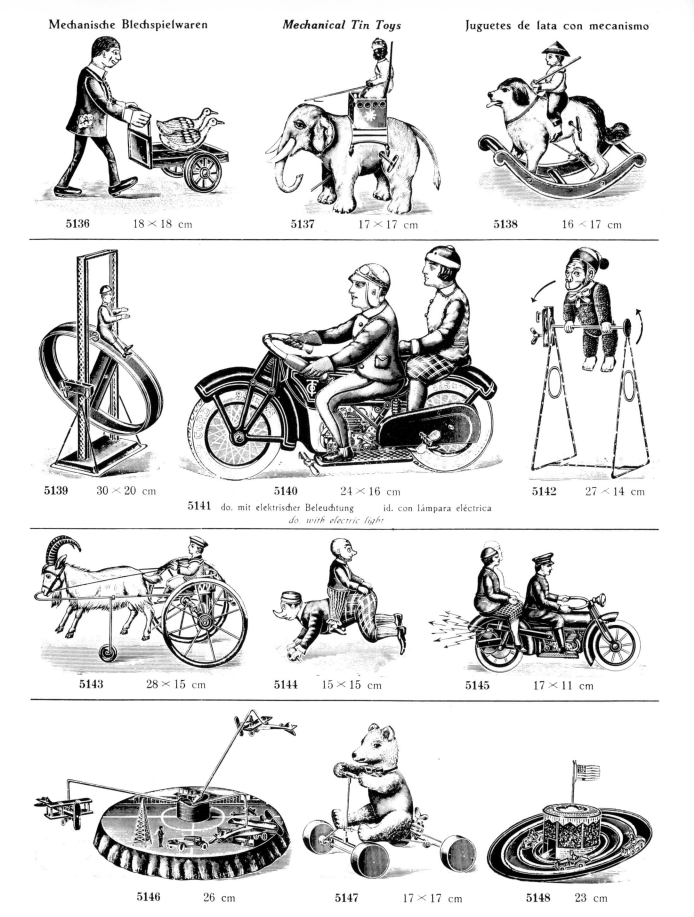

Mechanische Blechspielwaren   *Mechanical Tin Toys*   Juguetes de lata con mecanismo

5136   18 × 18 cm   **5137**   17 × 17 cm   **5138**   16 × 17 cm

5139   30 × 20 cm   **5140**   24 × 16 cm   **5142**   27 × 14 cm

5141   do. mit elektrischer Beleuchtung   id. con lámpara eléctrica
do. with electric light

5143   28 × 15 cm   **5144**   15 × 15 cm   **5145**   17 × 11 cm

5146   26 cm   **5147**   17 × 17 cm   **5148**   23 cm

Knapp Electric Novelty Co.
New York, U.S.A.
Founded in 1890 by David W. Knapp
Specialized in the manufacture of
electric model railways.

Koch & Hofmockel
Nuremberg, Germany
Founded in 1902
Manufactured a variety of tinplate toys.
Trademark: *Koho*

Köhler
Nuremberg, Germany
Founded in 1932 by Georg Köhler
Manufactured mechanical tinplate
animals before and after World
War II.
Trademark: *G.K.N.* in a triangle

Kohnstam
Furth, Germany
Founded in 1876 by Moses Kohnstam
Distributed a wide range of toys,
eventually having branches in
London, Milan and Brussels.
Trademark: *Moko*

Kraus & Co.
Nuremberg, Germany
Founded in 1910 by Josef Kraus

A page from the Moses Kohnstam (Moko)
catalogue of 1928 illustrating a multitude of
novelty toys. Kohnstam was a toy merchant,
not a manufacturer, and his vast stock came
from a number of German toy makers. The
motorcycle near the centre of the page, for
instance, is a product of the Tipp factory (the
company's trademark is clearly visible), and
the figure with two geese (*top left*) is a well-
known Distler toy.

Manufactured clockwork and electric
toy trains; *see also* Dorfan.
Trademark: *Fandor*; *J.K.Co.* or
J.K.Co.N.

Hans Krauss
Nuremberg, Germany
Trademark: *H.K.*

Krauss
Nuremberg, Germany
Founded in 1895 by Wilhelm Krauss
Manufactured tinplate novelties such
as carousels and other toys.
Trademark: *W.K.* in a circle

La Hotte St Nicholas
St Nicholas d'Ailiermont, France
Founded in 1938 by the Denis brothers
Manufactured animated toys and road
vehicles.
Trademark: A gearwheel, an elephant's
head and *La Hotte St Nicholas*

Lampugnani
Milan, Italy
Founded in 1901
Manufactured a variety of tinplate toys;
taken over by Alemanni (*q.v.*) in
1908.

Leeds Model Co.
Leeds, England
Founded in 1912 by R. F. Stedman
Made a wide range of gauge O model
railway locomotives and rolling
stock.

Lehmann
Brandenburg, Germany
Founded in 1881 by Ernst Paul
Lehmann

Prolific manufacturer of novelty toys,
many originally supplied with fly-
wheel mechanisms.
Trademark: *E.P.L.* or initials combined
to form an "e" within a bell-shape
representing a metal press

Levy
Nuremberg, Germany
Founded in 1920 by Georg Levy
Levy had partnered Kienberger (*q.v.*)
before establishing his own company
to manufacture a wide range of
novelty tinplate items.
Trademark: *Gely*

Linemar Toys
Tokyo, Japan
Founded c. 1950
Produced (or distributed) a variety of
animated novelty tinplate toys.

Lineol
Brandenburg, Germany
Founded in 1934
Specialized in manufacturing toy
military vehicles and composition
soldiers similar to Hausser's
Elastolin figures.
Trademark: A trio of ducks walking
heads-in-air

Lines Brothers
London, England
Founded in 1919 by Walter, Arthur and
William Lines
Manufactured tinplate and pressed-
steel toy vehicles and other toys.
Trademark: *Tri-ang* (registered 1927)
and *Minic* (registered in 1930s)

Lionel
New York, U.S.A.
Founded in 1906 by J. Lionel Cowan
Originally made a variety of toys,

specializing in model railways and accessories; after 1945 made railways only.
Trademark: *Lionel*

Lollini
Bologna, Italy
Founded in 1922 by Giovanni Lollini when he took over Rappini (*q.v.*) in 1922
Lollini continued manufacture of tin toys by Rappini.

Herman Löwenstein
Zürich, Switzerland
Founded in 1918
Produced model electric railways following shortage of German toys after World War I.
Trademark: *Ha, El* and *Zet* in the corner of a triangle

Lutz
Ellwangen an der Jagst, Germany
Founded *c.* 1846 by Ludwig Lutz
Made high quality tin toys – e.g., clockwork horse-drawn carriages, boats and trains; one of the companies bought by Märklin (*q.v.*), it was taken over in 1891.

G. H. Malins
Birmingham, England
Founded in 1936
Originally manufactured stationary steam engines but later made other steam toys; still in business.
Trademark: *Mamod*

ABOVE TOP
Maker **Possibly Maltête et Parent**
Marks **None**
Date *c.* 1890
Length 15¼in (39cm)
This early clockwork paddle-steamer may have been made by the French firm, Maltête et Parent, which made many toy ships, often with tiny figureheads. Examples are rare and, because they carry no trademark, can be recognized only by their graceful lines.
Sotheby's

ABOVE
Maker **Gama (Mangold)**
Marks *Gama 125 Made in U.S. Zone Germany*
Date **1950s**
Length 6¾in (17cm)
This ingenious little toy appeared in the 1950s, and it was produced by Gama, which was based in the U.S. Zone of Germany, the area occupied by American troops after World War II. The monkey driver manages to raise himself to a standing position on the top of the machine as it travels along and then resumes a sitting position. This is a novelty toy of great appeal: it is therefore scarce.

Maltête et Parent
Paris, France
Founded in 19th century by C. H. Maltête and G. Parent
Manufactured a very wide range of mechanical toys including a number of novelty toys, paddle-boats and submarines.

Mangold
Furth, Germany
Founded in 1882 by George Adam Mangold
Made toys under licence to Schuco (*q.v.*) in late 1940s.

Trademark: *GAMA* (from founder's name) used in early 1920s

Mansei Toy Company
Tokyo, Japan
Founded in 1951
Manufactured a wide range of novelty tinplate toys and novelty figures.
Trademark: *Haji* in a horizontal ellipse

A. Marchesini
Bologna, Italy
Founded in 1908 by Agostino Marchesini
Made penny toys.

L. Marchesini
Bologna, Italy
Founded in 1946 by a son of Agostino Marchesini (see above)
Noted for its quality products including a range of excellent model cars.

Maker **Märklin**
Marks *G.M. & Cie.* [intertwined] in a shield
Date **1905**
Length **13½in (34cm)**
Märklin made railway locomotives in all shapes and sizes. This one was obviously intended for the North American market, for this small gauge O locomotive sports a bell, a tall chimney and a cow catcher. It is an 0-4-0 live-steam engine, which has been well preserved because the paintwork on the boiler has not become blistered by the heat. A rare item.

Marescot
France
Founded in 1915
Made quality gauge O toy trains in liaison with Bassett-Lowke (*q.v.*); taken over by Fournereau (*q.v.*) in 1928.

Markes & Co. *see* Dux

Märklin
Göppingen, Germany
Founded in 1859 by Theodor Friedrich Wilhelm Märklin
Originally made children's cooking ranges; eventually became *the* name in the manufacture of quality tin-plate toys – boats, railways etc.
Trademark: *G.M. Cie* intertwined within a shield

Martin
Paris, France
Founded in 1878 by Fernand Martin
Produced a host of hand-painted tinplate novelty toys and figures with novelty actions. Taken over by Bonnet & Cie (*q.v.*) in 1912.
Trademark: *F.M.* in a circle

Marx
New York, U.S.A.
Founded in 1920 by Louis Marx
Became the largest toy manufacturer in the world. Marx bought out many other toy makers; had a factory in Britain in the 1930s.
Trademark: *Marx* and *Marlines*; circle with cross and *M.A.R.*

Masutoku Toy Factory *see* M. T. (Modern Toys)

Meccano *see* Hornby

Meier
Nuremberg, Germany
Founded in 1879 by Johann Philipp Meier
Noted for production of penny toys.
Trademark: Dog pulling a cart (registered in 1894) and *J.M.* monogram

Memo *see* Gutmann and S.F.A.

Merriam Manufacturing Co.
Durham, Connecticut, U.S.A.
Founded c. 1856
Manufactured a variety of tin toys until the end of the 19th century.
Trademark: none usually used

Metalgraf
Milan, Italy
Founded in 1910
Originally manufactured metal boxes, started making toys in 1920s and became noted for quality toys including fine toy cars; went out of business in 1930s.

Meteor
Netherlands
Operating during 1930s
Produced small, candle-powered tinplate steamboats, marked K21 and K30.
Trademark: *Meteor*

Mettoy
London, England
Founded in 1934 by Philipp Ullmann of Tipp & Co. (*q.v.*)
Made tinplate toys, especially cars and aircraft, similar to those produced by Tipp.
Trademark: *Mettoy* in the 1930s and 1940s; *Corgi* in the 1960s

Milton Bradley
Springfield, Massachusetts, U.S.A.

Founded c. 1860
Made optical and musical toys.
Trademark: *M.B.C.* in an oval

Minic *see* Lines Brothers
Moko *see* Kohnstam

Moline Pressed Steel Co.
East Moline, Illinois, U.S.A.
Made toys from pressed steel.
Trademark: *Buddy L*

Moschkowitz
Nuremberg, Germany
Founded c. 1919 by Max Moschkowitz
Produced a small number of tinplate clockwork toys, opened a branch in U.K. in 1929.
Trademark: *M.N.* in a circle

M.T. (Modern Toys)
Tokyo, Japan
Founded in 1924 by K. K. Masutoku
Produced a great variety of tin and celluloid toys; from 1950s made battery-operated novelty toys.
Trademark: *T.M.* monogram within a diamond

Müller & Kadeder
Nuremberg, Germany
Founded c. 1900
Manufactured animated tinplate clockwork toys.
Trademark: Hot-air balloon with *M.K.*

This fine model of a 1935 Junkers transport plane has been built from a Märklin construction set. It is 22in (56cm) long. The prototype aircraft was Germany's leading transport plane for many years – the equivalent of the U.S. Dakota – and the model is rare. *Sotheby's*

LEFT
Maker **Marx**
Marks *Marx*
Date **1930s**
The "Merry Makers", a tinplate American toy made by Louis Marx in the 1930s. A clockwork mechanism animates the figures and brings the toy to life. A popular toy and one that is often seen in collections, but it is difficult to find it actually for sale! *Sotheby's*

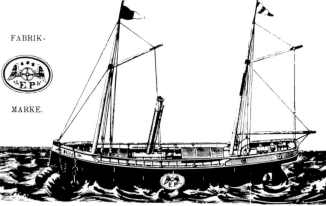

Schrauben-Dampfer
in neuer hochfeiner Ausführung.

FABRIK-

MARKE.

ABOVE
This illustration appeared in a catalogue published by Ernst Plank at the beginning of the century. It shows three attractive live-steam boats, 8¾in (22cm), 11¾in (30cm) and 23¾in (60cm) long respectively.

RIGHT
Maker   **Unknown (possibly Oro-Werke)**
Marks   *Made in Brandenburg*
Date   *c.*1910
Length **10in (26cm)**
This charming early motor bus, with its curtained windows and neatly scripted soap

advertisements, recalls the pre-World War I days. The maker is not known, although the *Made in Brandenburg* in small print on the side suggests that it may have been an early item from Oro-Werke. The steering is adjustable and the bus is very rare.

Musizza
Turin, Italy
Founded in 1911 by A. Musizza
Specialized in "scientific" toys – steam engines, electric motors, etc. – which led it into the manufacture of electric and steam locomotives.

Neil, Blechschmidt & Müller *see* Oro-Werke

Neuhierl
Fürth, Germany
Founded in 1920 by Joseph Neuhierl
Produced many tinplate toys both before and after World War II.
Trademark: *J.N.F.*

Nomura Toys *see* T.N.

Nüsslein
Zirndorf, Germany
Founded in 1889 by Michael Nüsslein
Manufactured humming-tops, music-

boxes, rolling bells and magic lanterns.
Trademark: Two lions supporting a top; *M.N.N.* in a circle

Oro-Werke (Neil, Blechschmidt & Müller)
Brandenburg, Germany
Made a range of cheaper tinplate toys of all kinds – cars, trams and other carpet toys – before and after World War I.
Trademark: *Orowerke* or *Orobr*

Orowerke

Orobr

Paya
Ibi and Alicante, Spain
Founded in 1906 by Hermaños [Brothers] Paya

Made toy trains and various tin mechanical toys; currently re-producing tinplate toys.
Trademark: *P.H., R.A.I.* or stylized *Paya* in shape of locomotive

Péan Frères
Paris, France
Manufactured metal toys of all kinds.
Trademark: *P.F.*

Plank

Nuremberg, Germany
Founded in 1866 by Ernst Plank
Main output was magic lanterns and
optical toys; also produced
stationary and locomotive steam
engines and road vehicles.
Trademark: Winged wheel above *E.P.*
within an oval

Radiguet

Paris, France
Founded in 1872
Specialized in well-made steamboats
and brass toy locomotives; in 1889
became Radiguet & Massiot.
Trademark: No special mark

Rappini

Bologna, Italy
Founded in 1897
Produced many tin toys, including a
number of toy cars; taken over by
Lollini (*q.v.*) in 1922.

M. Richard & Co.

Nuremberg, Germany
Founded *c.* 1928
Made tin toys, some of which appeared
in the Moko (*q.v.*) catalogues.
Trademark: A clown in a circle with
Ri-Co N.

Rico

Ibi, Spain
Founded in 1920
Manufactured tinplate mechanical

vehicles and other novelty toys; also
made dolls.
Trademark: *R.S.A.* with biplane or *Rico*

Rissman

Nuremberg, Germany
Founded in 1907 by William Rissman
(Ritzmann)
Took over the toy factory of M. Ettinger
and made train sets.
Trademark: Stylized *Wi. Ri.* in a shield

Rock & Graner

Biberach an der Riss, Germany
Founded in 1813
Produced many tin toys, including

horse-drawn vehicles and fine clockwork trains.
Trademark: Included initials *R. & G.N.*

Karl Rohrseitz
Zirndorf, Germany
Founded in 1881 by Karl Rohrseitz
After World War I made money-boxes, buckets and spades and humming-tops
Trademark: *K.R.Z.*

Roitel
Paris, France
Founded in 1880 by Charles Roitel
Made mechanical tin toys including cars and trams.
Trademark: *C.R.* intertwined (may be confused with Rossignol's cypher)

Rosenbauer
Nuremberg, Germany
Founded in 1900 by Karl Rosenbauer
Made tinplate toys, including model ships.
Trademark: *K.R.N.*

W. Rosenbauer
Nuremberg, Germany
Founded in 19th century

Known to have been in existence in 1860, produced ships and live steam model locomotives.

Rossignol
Paris, France
Founded in 1868 by Charles Rossignol
Made carpet (floor) trains, clockwork cars, Paris buses and fire-engines.
Trademark: *C.R.* (similar to Roitel)

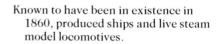

Rouissy
Paris, France
Founded in 1920s by Louis Rouissy
Made clockwork and electric toy railways; advertised "the fastest model trains in the world".
Trademark: *L.R.*

Maker **Rossignol**
Marks *C.R.*
Date **1910–20**
Length **12in (31cm)**
This gilded tinplate locomotive is a clockwork "carpet toy", evocative of the early days of the railways. It is a product of the French firm Charles Rossignol, which made a range of these particular toys. They are not easy to find in the U.K., although, as one would expect, examples turn up more often in France.

Saalheimer & Strauss
Nuremberg, Germany
Founded in 1912, taken over by Philipp
    Niedermeier in 1934
Little is known of the products of this
    company.
Trademark: *S.S.* intertwined in a
    circle; after 1934 the Nuremberg
    tower

Sakai
Japan
Founded in 1930s
Made electric model railways.
Trademark: *Seki*

San
Tokyo, Japan
Made lithographed tinplate toys.

Schoenner produced this finely detailed live-steam locomotive in 75mm gauge in the early part of the century. The locomotive was 18in (46cm) long, and the tender was 13in (33cm) long.

Gebrüder Schmid
Nuremberg, Germany
Trademark: *Gescha* or *G.S.N.*

Schoenner
Nuremberg, Germany
Founded in 1875 by Jean Schoenner
Made steam trains, engines and boats;
    also clockwork toys.
Trademark: *J.S.* with a star and a wheel

Schreyer & Co. (Schuco)
Nuremberg, Germany
Founded in 1912 by Herr Schreyer and
    Heinrich Muller
Produced an amazing variety of novelty
    toys as well as some soft toys.
Trademark: *Schuco*

Schrödel
Nuremberg, Germany
Founded in 1846 by Johann Schrödel
Originally book-binders, began to
    manufacture games in 1848,
    specializing in shooting games.
Trademark: *Ideal*

Schroeder & Co.
Ludenscheid, Germany
Producer of steam engines.
Trademark: *Wilesco*

Schuco *see* Schreyer & Co.

A. Schuhmann
Nuremberg, Germany
Probably founded before 1914
Manufactured model railways and
    tinplate toy motor cars.
Trademark: *A.S.* or *A.S.N.*

Secor
Bridgeport, Connecticut, U.S.A.
Founded in 1880 by Jerome B. Secor
Made automata, singing birds,
    novelties and so on, often with
    musical movements.

Seidel
Nuremberg, Germany
Founded in 1881 by Max Seidel
Made money-boxes (still banks), tea-
sets and later boats, tanks, etc.
Trademark: Rampant goat with *M.S.*

S.F.A. (Société de Fabrication et d'Assemblage)
Moutreuil, France
Founded in 1936
See also Gutmann.
Trademarks: *Memo, Jouet Bouree* and
S.F.A. Paris in a triangle

S.H. *see* Horikawa Toys

S.I.F. (Société Industrielle de Ferblanterie)
Paris, France
Founded in 1898
Produced toys for many other French
manufacturers, including C.I.J.

(*q.v.*). Became J.E.P. (*q.v.*)
Trademark: *S.I.F.*

Staudt
Nuremberg, Germany
Founded *c.*1860 by Leonhard Staudt
Made mechanical toys – clockwork
roundabouts with small airplanes
and zeppelins. Taken over by
Fleischmann (*q.v.*) in 1936.
Trademark: Circle with a sketch of a
village and *St.*

Stevens & Brown Manufacturing Co.
Connecticut, U.S.A.
Founded in 1868
Formed by the merger of George W.
Brown & Co. (*q.v.*) and J. & E.
Stevens, makers of cast-iron toys;
manufactured tinplate dolls' house
furniture.
Trademark: none usually used

Stock & Co.
Solingen, Germany
Founded in 1905 by Walter Stock
Manufactured tinplate Christmas items
as well as toys; also made toy cars
and toys in the style of Lehmann
(*q.v.*).
Trademark: *Stock*; two crossed
walking-sticks (*Stock* is German for
walking-stick) in a circle

Ferdinand Strauss
Rutherford, New Jersey, U.S.A.
Founded in early 20th century
A leading manufacturer of U.S.
mechanical, wind-up toys; the
company was taken over by Marx
(*q.v.*) *c.*1920.

Sutcliffe Pressings Ltd
Horsforth, Leeds, England
Founded in 1885; made toy boats
from 1920
Manufactured good quality toy boats:
first examples had spirit-fired water-
circulatory engines but later models
driven by clockwork.
Trademark: *Sutcliffe*

Front ship
Maker **Sutcliffe**
Marks *Sutcliffe Horsforth England*
Date **1920s**
Length **16in (41cm)**

Rear ship
Maker **Sutcliffe**
Marks *Sutcliffe*
Date **1920s**
Length **16in (41cm)**

These two early Sutcliffe battleships were
known as the *Nelson*. The ship in front is the
earlier of the two and has the "toc-toc"
motor operated by a spirit burner. The
other is a clockwork version, and it has two
extra gun turrets, one on each side. These
models are becoming harder to find as
interest in this company's products grows.
Mike Butler collection

NAUTILUS
the SUBMARINE from Walt Disney's
'20,000 LEAGUES UNDER THE SEA'
by Jules Verne

A clockwork submarine that dives and surfaces automatically

EACH MODEL TESTED AND GUARANTEED

COPYRIGHT WALT DISNEY PRODUCTIONS

MADE IN ENGLAND

Maker **Sutcliffe**
Marks *Sutcliffe*
Date **1978**
Length **9in (23cm)**

Sutcliffe's *Nautilus* submarine was one of the "clones" of the firm's popular *Unda-Wunda* (the other was *The Sea Wolf*). This toy was produced in conjunction with the Walt Disney movie *20,000 Leagues Under the Sea*, and it was manufactured as recently as 1978. An interesting accessory is one of the specially designed shop-window showcards, which makes a fascinating 3-D presentation of the model. It is becoming increasingly difficult to find this toy in good condition, and its Disney association adds interest for another group of collectors.

Taiyo Kogyo Ltd
Tokyo, Japan
Founded in 1959
Produced a range of tinplate toys
during the 1960s.
Trademark: A "stick robot" figure with
Taiyo

Technofix *see* Gebrüder Einfalt

Tipp & Co.
Nuremberg, Germany
Founded in 1912 by Miss Tipp and
Mr Carstens

Prolific toy manufacturers famed
especially for cars; the proprietor,
Phillip Ullmann, fled from the Nazis
and founded Mettoy (*q.v.*) in 1934.
Trademark: *T. Co.* intertwined or
Tippco

T.N. (Nomura Toys)
Tokyo, Japan
Founded in 1923
An older Japanese firm, which
produced a range of tinplate
novelties after World War II.
Trademark: *T.N.* in a diamond

T.P.S. (Toplay)
Tokyo, Japan
Founded in 1956
Made a range of novelty tin toys.
Trademark: Hand with three raised
fingers with *T.P.S.* in a scroll

Tri-ang *see* Lines Brothers

Trix
Nuremberg, Germany
Founded in 1927
Made the popular construction sets and
introduced 16.5mm gauge electric
trains; an English subsidiary was
established in 1935.
Trademark: *Trix*

LEFT
Maker **Tipp & Co.**
Marks *TCO* monogram
Date 1960s
Length 9¾in (25cm)
A product of the German company, Tipp &
Co., this tinplate fire-engine with an
extending ladder is powered by a simple
friction mechanism. These post-war
examples were well produced. Specialist
fire-engine collectors soon buy up any of the
toys produced in this form, and although this
particular model is not especially rare, it
could be hard to come across if you needed
to buy one to complete a collection.

RIGHT
Maker **Whiteley, Tansley & Co.**
Marks *Whitanco L.* [in a wheel]
Date 1920–30
Length 5in (13cm)
Whiteley, Tansley & Co. was a company of
toy makers founded in 1916 in Liverpool,
England, which made interesting tinplate
vehicles such as this decorative clockwork
truck. After World War I the company also
produced toy trains. This company's
products are not easy to find, although they
do turn up at toy fairs from time to time.

Ubilda *see* Chad Valley and Burnett

Uebelacker
Nuremberg, Germany
Founded *c.*1860 by Leonhard
    Uebelacker; in 1934 Christian
    Uebelacker began toy making and
    could be connected
Made toy ships and aircraft.
Trademark: Neptune in chariot drawn
    by sea-horse within an oval

Ullmann & Engelmann
Furth, Germany
Manufactured novelty tin toys, model
    railways, boats, scientific toys and
    steam toys.

Union Manufacturing Co.
Connecticut, U.S.A.
Founded in 1853
Manufactured tin toys; acquired by
    Hull & Stafford (*q.v.*) in 1869.

Usagiya
Tokyo, Japan
Founded in 1950
Produced tinplate novelty toys.
Trademark: A rabbit's face with
    elongated ear

V.E.B. Mechanishe Spielwaren
Brandenburg, Germany
Founded in 1944
The successor of Lehmann (*q.v.*);
    manufactured tinplate novelties.
Trademark: *V.E.B.* in a circle or
    stylized *M.S.* in a circle

Vielmetter
Germany
Founded *c.*1897 by Philip Vielmetter
Apparently made just one toy – "The
    Artist" – which draws caricatures
    through interchangeable, hand-
    operated cams.

Volkseigener Betreib Mechanic
Brandenburg, Germany
Founded *c.*1947
The successors to Lehmann (*q.v.*)
    making a variety of mechanical tin
    toys.
Trademark: Circular logo with *V.E.B.*,
    also *M* logo in a circle

Voltamp Electric Manufacturing Co.
Baltimore, U.S.A.
Founded in 1903 by M. E. Fold
Manufactured electric model railways
and trains.

Weedon Manufacturing Co.
Boston, Massachusetts, U.S.A.
Founded in 1882
Made model steam-powered ships and
locomotives and electric gauge O
model railways.

Wells & Co
London, England
Founded in 1923
Made aircraft, cars, buses, etc., in
tinplate; took over Brimtoy (*q.v.*) to
form Wells-Brimtoy in 1932.
Trademark: Two water wells

Whiteley, Tansley & Co.
Liverpool, England
Founded before 1916
Manufactured small range of tinplate
road vehicles and trains.
Trademark: Ornamental wheel with
Whitanco (registered in 1916)

Wilkins
New Hampshire, U.S.A.
Founded in 1888 by James Wilkins
Made cast-iron toys; financial problems
led to sell out to Harry T. Kingsbury
(*q.v.*).

Wimmer
Nuremberg, Germany
Founded in 1928 by Heinrich Wimmer
Made clockwork cars, aircraft, trains,
animals, etc.; toy trains only made
from 1950.
Trademark: *H.W.N.* in a scroll

Wolverine Manufacturing Co.
Pittsburgh, U.S.A.
Founded c.1910
Produced mechanical toys operated by
gravity such as "Sandy Andy", a sand
toy.
Trademark: Company name

Yoneya Toys Co. Ltd
Tokyo, Japan
Founded in 1950
Made a wide range of tinplate toys
throughout the 1950s and 1960s.
Trademark: *Yone*

Yonezawa Toys Co. Ltd
Tokyo, Japan
Founded in 1950s
Produced variety of battery-operated
tinplate and plastic toys.
Trademark: *Y* in a stylized flower-head

INDEX OF TRADEMARKS

Anfoe	Förtner & Haffner, Nuremberg
A.S. *or* **A.S.N.**	Adolf Schuhmann, Nuremberg
A.S.G.W.	S. Günthermann, Nuremberg
A.T.C.	Asahi Toy Co., Tokyo
B. & S.	Blomer & Schüler, Nuremberg
Betal	J. H. Glasman Ltd. London.
Brimtoy	Wells & Co., London
Buco	A. Bücherer, Diepoldsau, Switzerland
B.W.	Bing-Werke, Nuremberg
C.K. *or* **C.K.O.**	Georg Kellermann, Nuremberg
Codeg	Cowan de Groot, U.K.
C.R.	Charles Roitel, Paris *or* Charles Rossignol, Paris
D.C.	Doll & Cie., Nuremberg
Dux	Markes & Co., Lüdenscheidt
Efzet	Gustav Fischer, Zöblitz
E.H.N.	Emil Hausmann, Nuremberg
Elastolin	O. & M. Hausser, Neustadt
E.P.	Ernst Plank, Nuremberg
E.P.L.	Ernst Paul Lehmann, Brandenburg
Fandor	Josef Kraus, Nuremberg
F.M.	Fernand Martin, Paris
F.N.N.	Fritz Neumeyer, Nuremberg
F.V.	Edmond Faivre, Paris
Gama	Georg Adam Mangold, Nuremberg
G.B.N.	Gebrüder Bing, Nuremberg
G.C. & Co. *or* **G.C.Co.N** *or* **G.C.N.** *or* **G.C.N. Co.**	Georges Carette, Nuremberg
Gely	George Levy, Nuremberg
G.E.M.	Biaggi
G.E.N.	Gebrüder Einfalt, Nuremberg
Geobra	Georg Brandstätter, Nuremberg
Gescha	Gebrüder Schmid, Nuremberg
G.F.N.	Gebrüder Fleischmann, Nuremberg
G. & K.	Greppert & Kelch (Gundka-Werke), Brandenburg
G.K.N.	George Köhler, Nuremberg
G.M.C. *or* **G.M. & Cie.** *or* **G.M. & Co.** *or* **G.M.**	Gebrüder Märklin, Göppingen
G.N.K.	Georg Köhler, Nuremberg
Göso	Christian Götz & Son, Fürth
G.S.N.	Gebrüder Schmid, Nuremberg
Haji	Mansei Toy Co., Tokyo
H.E.N.	Hans Eberl, Nuremberg
Hessmobiel	Mattheus Hess, Nuremberg
H.K.	Hans Krauss, Nuremberg
Hornby	Meccano Ltd, Liverpool
H.P. *or* **H.Pai**	Hermaños Paya, Ibi
Huki	Hubert Kienberger, Nuremberg
Husch	Heller & Schiller, Obersleutensdorf
H.W.N.	Heinrich Wimmer, Nuremberg
I.B. & Co. *or* **I.B. & W. Co.**	Ives, Blakeslee & Co., Bridgeport, Connecticut
Ideal	J. G. Schrödel, Nuremberg
I.M.C.	Ives Manufacturing Co., Bridgeport, Connecticut
I. & W. Co.	Ives & Williams Co., Bridgeport, Connecticut
J.A.J.	Johann A. Issmayer, Nuremberg
J.D.N.	Johann Distler, Nuremberg
J.F. *or* **J.F.N.**	Joseph Falk, Nuremberg
J.F.J.	Fournereau, Paris
J.H.	Jean Höfler, Fürth
J.K. Co. *or* **J.K. Co. N.**	Josef Kraus, Nuremberg
J.L.H.	Johann Leonhard Hess, Nuremberg
J.M.	Johann Philipp Meier, Nuremberg
J.N.F.	Josef Neuhierl, Fürth
J. Ph. M.	Johann Philipp Meier, Nuremberg
J.S.	Jean Schoenner, Nuremberg
Jumbo	Blomer & Schüler, Nuremberg
K.B. *or* **K.B.N.**	Karl Bub, Nuremberg
K.B./B.W.	Karl Bub and Bing-Werke, Nuremberg (after 1933)
K. & B.B.	Kindler & Briel, Böblingen
K. Co.	Georg Kellermann, Nuremberg
Kibri	Kindler & Briel, Böblingen
Kico	Hubert Kienberger, Nuremberg
K.R.N.	Karl Rosenbaum, Nuremberg
K.R.Z.	Karl Rohrseitz, Zirndorf
L. Bros.	Lines Brothers Ltd, London
L.B.Z.	Lorenz Bolz, Zirndorf
Lowko	Bassett-Lowke, Northampton
Marlines	Louis Marx & Co., New York
M.B.	Milton Bradley, Springfield, Massachusetts
Memo	Mery Gutmann, Paris
Mettoy	Mettoy Playthings, Northampton
M.F.Z.	Martin Fuchs, Zirndorf
M.H.N.	Mattheus Hess, Nuremberg
M.K.	Müller & Kadeder, Nuremberg
M.L.D.L.	Meccano Ltd, Liverpool
M.M.N.	Max Moschkowitz, Nuremberg
M.N.N.	Michael Nüsslein, Nuremberg
M.D.	Michael Seidel, Nuremberg

M.T.	Masutoku Toy Factory, Tokyo	**Technofix**	Gebrüder Einfalt, Nuremberg (after c.1935)
New York Flyer	Hafner Manufacturing Co., Chicago		
Oro *or* **Orobr**	Oro-Werke (Neil, Blechschmidt & Müller), Brandenburg	**T.N.**	Nomura Toys, Tokyo
		T.P.S.	Toplay Ltd, Tokyo
P.F.	Péan Frères, Paris	**Tri-ang**	Lines Brothers Ltd, London
P.U.	Ichiko Kogyo Co., Tokyo	**Trix**	Trix Ltd, London *or* Trix, Nuremberg
P.V.	Philipp Vielmetter, Germany	**Ubilda**	Chad Valley, Nuremberg
Rai	Hermaños Paya, Ibi	**V.B. & Cie.** *or* **Vébé**	Victor Bonnet, Paris
R. & G.N.	Rock & Graner, Nuremberg		
Rapido	Karl Arnold, Nuremberg	**Whitanco**	Whiteley, Tansley & Co., Liverpool
Ri-co	Richard & Co., Nuremberg	**W.K.**	Wilhelm Krauss, Nuremberg
R.S.A.	Rico, Ibi	**W.R.**	William Rissman (Ritzmann), Nuremberg
Schuco	Schreyer & Co., Nuremberg		
S.G.	S. Günthermann, Nuremberg	**W. St.**	Walter Stock, Solingen
S.H.	Horikawa Toys, Tokyo	**Y.**	Yonezawa Toys Co., Tokyo
T. Co. *or* **Tippco**	Tipp & Co., Nuremberg	**Yone**	Yoneya Toys Co., Tokyo

Maker **Unknown English**
Marks **None**
Date **1920s**
Length **9½in (24cm)**
This 1920s bus was designed to hold samples of the biscuits produced by Huntley & Palmers. Tins such as this were not produced by toy makers but by various sheet metal companies specializing in the production of decorative metal boxes. This example is splendidly lithographed in great detail, but these novelty tins, when shaped as vehicles, were rarely, if ever, fitted with drive mechanisms.

BIBLIOGRAPHY

Adburgham, Alison (ed.), *Gamage's Christmas Bazaar, 1913*, David & Charles, Newton Abbot, Devon, 1974

Ayres, William S., *The Warner Collector's Guide to American Toys*, The Main Street Press, Warner Books Inc., New York, 1981

Baecker, Carlernst and Hass, Dieter, *Die Anderen Nürnberger* (7 volumes), Hobby Haas Verlag, Frankfurt am Main, 1973–81

Baecker, Carlernst, Hass, Dieter and Jeanmaire, Claude, *Technical Toys in the Course of Time*

    Volume 1: *Märklin (1859–1902): From the Foundation to the Turn of the Century,* Hobby Haas Verlag, Frankfurt am Main, 1975

    Volume 2: *Märklin (1904–1908): In the Emperor's Time, up to 1908*, Hobby Haas, 1976

    Volume 3: *Märklin (1891–1915): The Toy Railways from 1891 until 1915*, Verlag Eisenbahn, 1979

    Volume 4: *Märklin (1909–1912): New Ways to Success up to 1912*, Hobby Haas, 1978

    Volume 5: *Karl Arnold; Moses Kohnstam (Moko); Karl Bub; R. & G.N.; Georges Carette; Schreyer & Co. (Schuco)*, Hobby Haas 1976

    Volume 6: *Märklin (1919–1921): New Horizons up to 1921*, Hobby Haas, 1980

    Volume 7: *Märklin (1923–1927): The New Sales Catalogues*, Hobby Haas, 1981

    Volume 8: to be published

    Volume 9: *Märklin (1928–1929): The Golden Twenties*, Hobby Haas, 1983

    Volume 10: *Märklin (1902–1978): The Small Gauges OO/HO*, Verlag Eisenbahn, 1979

Baecker, Carlernst and Jeanmaire, Claude, *Technical Toys in the Course of Time* Volume 11: *Märklin: (1930–1931) Focus on the Reichsbahn*, Hobby Haas Verlag, Frankfurt am Main, 1984

Baecker, Carlernst and Väterlein, Christian, *Vergessenes Blechspielzeug (Germany's Forgotten Toymakers)*, Frankfurter Fachbuchhandlung Michael Kohl, Frankfurt am Main, 1982

Barenholtz, Bernard and McClintock, Inez, *American Antique Toys*, Harry N. Abrams, New York/New Cavendish Books, London, 1980

Bartholomew, Charles, *Mechanical Toys*, Hamlyn Publishing Group, Feltham, Middlesex, 1979

Becher, Udo, *Early Tinplate Model Railways*, V.E.B. Verlag für Verkehrswesen, 1979; Argus Books, Hemel Hempstead, Hertfordshire, 1980

Boogaerts, Pierre, *Robots*, Futuropolis, Paris, 1978

Bossi, Marco, *Autohobby*, Priuli & Verlucca, Ivrea, Italy, 1975

Carlson, Pierce, *Toy Trains: A History*, Harper & Row, New York/Victor Gollancz Ltd, London 1986

Cieslik, Jürgen and Marianne, *Lehmann Toys*, New Cavendish Books, London, 1982

Culff, Robert, *The World of Toys*, Hamlyn Publishing Group, Feltham, Middlesex, 1969

Daiken, Leslie, *Children's Toys Throughout the Ages*, Spring Books, London, 1963

Daiken, Leslie, *World of Toys*, Lambarda Press, London, 1963

Flick, Pauline, *Discovering Toy Museums*, Shire Publications, Tring, Hertfordshire, 1971

Franklin, M. J., *British Biscuit Tins*, New Cavendish Books, London, 1979

Gardiner, Gordon and Morris, Alistair, *Metal Toys*, Salamander Books, London, 1984

Gardiner, Gordon and O'Neill, Richard, *Toy Cars*, Salamander Books, London, 1985

Gomm, P. G., *Older Locomotives 1900–1942*, Thomas Nelson, Walton-on-Thames, 1970

Griffith, David, *Decorative Printed Tins: The Golden Age of Printed Tin Packaging*, Studio Vista, London, 1979

Harley, Basil, *Toyshop Steam*, Model and Allied Publications, Argus Books, Hemel Hempstead, Hertfordshire, 1978

Harley, Basil, *Toy Boats*, Shire Publications, Princes Risborough, Aylesbury, Buckinghamshire, 1987

Harrer, Kurt, *Lexikon Blech Spielzeug*, Alba Buchverlag GmbH & Co., Düsseldorf, 1982

Herscher, Georges, *L'Art et les Biscuits*, Editions du Chène, Paris, 1978

Hertz, Louis, H., *The Toy Collector*, Hawthorn Books/ Thomas Y. Crowell Co., 1967; Funk & Wagnalls, New York, 1969

Hervé, Gilles and Parry-Crooke, Charlotte (ed.), *Great Toys: Märklin 1895–1914*, Denys Ingram Publishers, London/Editions d'Art Monelle Hayot, Paris/ Orell Füssli Verlag, Zurich, 1983

Hillier, Mary, *Automata & Mechanical Toys: An Illustrated History*, Jupiter Books, London, 1976

Huntingdon, Bernard, *Along Hornby Lines*, Oxford Publishing Co., Oxford, 1976

Joyce, J., *Collectors' Guide to Model Railways*, Model and Allied Publications, Argus Books, Hemel Hempstead, Hertfordshire, 1977

Kelley, Dale, *Collecting the Tin Toy Car*, Schiffer Publishing Ltd, Exton, Pennsylvania, 1984

Kimball, Ward, *Toys: Delights from the Past*, Applied Arts Publishers, 1978

Marchand, F., *Motos-Jouets*, L'Automobiliste, Paris, 1985

McCrindell, Ron, *Toy Trains*, Salamander Books, London, 1985

Moran, Brian, *Battery Toys*, Schiffer Publishing Ltd, Exton, Pennsylvania, 1986

Murray, Patrick, *Toys*, Studio Vista, London, 1968

Parry-Crooke, Charlotte (ed.), *Mr Gamage's Great Toy Bazaar (1902–1906)*, Denys Ingram Publishers, London/Hastings House Publishers Inc., New York, 1982

Pressland, David, *The Art of the Tin Toy*, New Cavendish Books, London, 1976

Pressland, David (consultant), *Toy Autos 1890–1939: The Peter Ottenheimer Collection*, Denys Ingram Publishers, London, 1984

Rampini, Paolo, *Encyclopedia of Toy Cars*, Rampini, Milan, 1984

Rampini, Paolo, *Le Auto-Giocattolo Italiane*, Rampini, Milan, 1986

Randall, P. E., *Recent Locomotives 1947–1970*, Thomas Nelson, Walton-on-Thames, 1970

Remise, Jac and Frederick, *Attelages, Automobiles et Cycles*, Edita-Vilo, Lausanne, 1985

Remise, Jac and Frederic, *Les Bâteaux*, Pygmalion, Paris, 1982

Remise, Jac and Fondin, Jean, *The Golden Age of Toys*, Edita S.A., Lausanne, 1967

Ricci, F. M., *Androids*, Scriptar S.A., Lausanne, 1979

Richardson, S., *Minic*, Mikansue, Windsor, 1981

Société des Amis du Jouet, *Jouets*, Paris, 1984

Thompson, R., *Hornby Silhouette: Whispers of Childhood* (video), Thompson, Sale, Cheshire, 1984

Weltens, Arno, *Mechanical Tin Toys in Colour*, Blandford Press, Poole, Dorset, 1977

SPECIALIST MAGAZINES

Antique Toy World, published monthly, by subscription only.

U.S.A.: Dale Kelley, Box 34509, Chicago, IL 60634 (tel: 312-725-0633)

Europe: A.T.W., 46 Grangethorpe Drive, Manchester, M19 2LQ (tel: 061-224-8960)

Collectors' Gazette, published monthly. On sale at swap meets and by subscription.

Martin Weiss, 92 Kirkby Road, Sutton-in-Ashfield, Nottingham, NG17 1GH (tel: 0623-515574)

INDEX

Page numbers in *italics* refer to captions to illustrations.